The Poetical Books
(Job, Psalms, & Proverbs)

By Mrs. T. M. Constance

Book 3 - Lessons 21 - 31

We believe the Bible is God's Word, a divine revelation, in the original language
verbally inspired in its entirety, and that it is the supreme infallible authority
in all matters of faith and conduct.
(II Peter 1:21; II Timothy 3:16)

Printed in the United States of America

Published by Explorer's Bible Study
2652 Hwy. 46 South
P.O. Box 425
Dickson, TN 37056-0425
1-615-446-7316

Psalms 106-118

Introduction

The Psalter is divided into five books:

Book I: Psalms 1-41
Book II: Psalms 42-72
Book III: Psalms 73-89
Book IV: Psalms 90-106
Book V: Psalms 107-150

It is remarkable that in these historical psalms, there is an absence of anything that would tend to feed national vanity. All the glory of Israel's history is due to God's mercy and blessing. All the failures written of, losses, reverses, the sword, famine and exile, are recognized as the righteous chastisement which the sin of the nation provoked.

I.   Psalm 106

The author of this psalm is not known. The time period in which it was written probably was during the days when Israel was in captivity in Babylon. It is the closing psalm of the fourth book of Psalms and is a companion to Psalm 105. Psalm 105 relates how God treated Israel and His faithfulness to His people. Psalm 106 tells how Israel treated God and their unfaithfulness to Him. Both psalms give a summarization of the history of Israel. Psalm 105 celebrates the mighty acts of God for His people with joy. In Psalm 106, the burden of sin is confessed humbly by the people. It begins and ends with the words: *"Praise the Lord."*

This psalm has four divisions.

1. Verses 1-5: Introduction

2. Verses 6-33: The history of Israel from Egypt and through the wilderness—a history of perpetual transgressions.

3. Verses 34-46: In the Holy land.

4. Verse 47: Conclusion - prayer for deliverance from the captivity in Babylon.

"Praise the Lord. Oh, give thanks to the Lord, for He is good! For His mercy endures forever." The two reasons for praise are themselves praise. The praise is for God's mercy to His chosen people which endures from generation to generation. This first verse is the subject of all that follows.

The psalmist prayed for himself. The salvation he desired to share was the deliverance from exile (verse 47).

"Blessed are those who keep justice, And he who does righteousness at all times!" (verse 3). Principles and practices are involved in true praise. Thanks-doing is the proof of thanksgiving. The life of the thankful is the life of thankfulness. "Praise the Lord" must be said with heart-meaning. To say "Praise the Lord" without really thinking about what the praise is for is the utterance of words with no meaning. Unless our words of praise come from the heart, our Lord can not accept them. What a beautiful thing it is to feel so blessed by the Lord, that the words, "Praise the Lord" come spontaneously from the lips. Grateful and thankful hearts cannot help but praise Him. Psalm 107 expresses this in several verses. *"Oh, that men would give thanks to the Lord for His goodness, and for His wonderful works to the children of men!"* Psalm 106:7 says, *"Our fathers in Egypt did not understand Your wonders; they did not remember the multitude of Your mercies...."* God's people did not understand the things done by Him for their deliverance. There is a real danger, even for us today, to take God's blessings for granted and to not consider the source of all blessing. It was God who manifested Himself on behalf of the children of Israel in dividing the Red Sea, in making a dry path, and destroying the enemy. Yet, how soon did their

religious enthusiasm, faith and feeling pass away? In the wilderness, they tempted God and He gave them what they asked for, but they also lost something that was better than the supplement to their diet. In Numbers 11:31-34, due to their greediness, God sent a plague and many died. The psalm says that God sent leanness to their souls. Our mercies may be our curses. A consistent temptation is that of placing our confidence in things that are in sight and within reach. The more these things multiply, the greater our danger becomes of placing our trust in things. If we have placed our trust in things, they have become our gods. Power and success can be a fearful thing.

Another symptom of spiritual leanness and the result of having our desires is self-pleasing. The pursuit of pleasure, or happiness, is a god that is never satisfied and flits from one place or thing to another as we chase after it. Pleasure-seeking is one of the most popular gods of our day, and the more we pursue this god, the more it becomes the aim and business of life. We shrink from things that call for self-sacrifice. There is a loss of sympathy with all that helps to build up the spiritual life. Let us be sensitive to the truth that we cannot be obsessed in our prayers, or in our desires, for only the temporal things in life. They can be the means of leanness to our souls.

The children of Israel worshipped the god of self-pleasing. The fruits of this worship were envy, outward worship of a golden calf, murmuring, following a false prophet and unbelief. These kept them from the promised land and caused them to wander for 40 years in the wilderness. In worshipping the god of self-pleasing, they missed the joy and pleasure which God had planned for them. The punishment of the older generation was to die in the wilderness. Their descendants, because of sin and disobedience, died in the dispersion and captivity among the Gentiles. To remember all that might have been, had they been obedient to God, must have been devastating to the Jews in Babylon. Phinehas, because of an act of zeal for the Lord, was rewarded with perpetual priesthood. His was an act that had its origin in faithfulness that had its root in faith.

After entering the land of Canaan, the children of Israel spared the nations that God had told them to destroy. Also against God's command, they mingled among the people of these heathen nations. As a result, their lives became intertwined with the heathen. They began worshipping idols. They sacrificed their children to heathen gods and devils, adding murder to their idolatry. We think of their shedding of innocent infant blood with horror. They defiled not only the land of promise, but themselves.

During their captivity in Babylon, the children of Israel remembered the sins of their forefathers. They remembered and God remembered. Verse 47 is their prayer, *"Save us, O Lord our God, and gather us from among the Gentiles, to give thanks to Your holy name, to triumph in Your praise."*

"Nevertheless (even upon remembering all the times and ways in which they had forsaken Him) *He regarded their affliction, When He heard their cry; and for their sake He remembered His covenant, and relented according to the multitude of His mercies."*

This psalm closes with a call for all the people to say, "Amen." It is the conclusion of the prayers and praise of God's people. Luther said, "As your Amen is, so has been your prayer."

II. Psalm 107

This psalm is the beginning of Book Five of the Psalter which is the last collection of psalms. This psalm celebrates the kindness of the Lord to those wandering in the wilderness, to those sitting in darkness and captivity; to those in affliction and sickness, to those in a storm at sea and to those who return with repentance to the Lord under any corrective visitation.

"Let the redeemed of the Lord say so." "Redeemed from what?" some may ask. The people of God are redeemed from the curse of the law, the powers of sin and darkness and the bondage of corruption. People are gathered by His grace from every nation, kindred, people and tongue. All are to give God praise because He truly has given deliverance from the hand of the enemy. Trials bring us to God in prayer. Through prayer and believing, God has redeemed us. We are given assurance that He will be with us and carry us through difficult times. We can conclude, as did the Psalmist in verse 7, *"And He led them forth by the right way."* The redeemed

can say, "God **for** us, God **with** us, and God **in** us." The indwelling of God is our salvation.

The psalmist gives four examples of man's perils and the goodness of God in providing deliverance from them. The four examples of distress mentioned here are taken from a broad spectrum of human experiences. The psalmist also calls on those who have experienced God's care and protection to praise the Lord for His goodness. There is no doubt as to the great lesson which this psalm teaches. It teaches us not only that God's providence watches over us, but that His ear is open to our prayers. It teaches us that prayer may be sought for temporal deliverance and that such prayer is answered. It teaches us that it is right to acknowledge answers to our prayers with thanksgiving.

A. First Example of Distress - Wandering in the Wilderness (Verses 4-9)

When the children of Israel came out of Egypt, they wandered in the wilderness instead of entering into the Holy Land. There were many troubles and privations. Had it not been for the pillar of cloud by day and the pillar of fire by night, they would have lost their way. So it is with Christians today. There are times when the circumstances of our lives make us feel as if we are wandering in a wilderness. There are many troubles and privations in the journey of life, but we have Christ as our guide day by day as we trust Him. He has promised to guide us by His counsel so we will not lose our way. In answer to our prayers, He will give us wisdom for direction and sustain us by His Word and by the Holy Spirit.

B. Second example of Distress - Brought Down with Labor (Verses 10-16)

"Therefore He brought down their heart with labor; they fell down, and there was none to help." Affliction was in full measure. They were in a position of helplessness and had become aware that there was no hope or help apart from God. For many, this circumstance reminds us of the time before we knew Christ. We had to come to that place of recognizing that we could not save ourselves. There is salvation in no other than Christ. *"Then they cried out to the Lord in their trouble, and He saved them out of their distresses"* (verse 13).

C. Third example of Distress - Afflicted with Sickness (verses 17-22)

"Fools, because of their transgression, and because of their iniquities, were afflicted." Many sicknesses are a direct result of foolish acts. God has endowed man with what we refer to as "common sense." In spite of the medical knowledge available, if we deliberately go against that which we know is not in the best interest of good health habits, we generally reap the results of sickness at some stage of our life. You hear people say, "It's none of your business as to what I choose in personal habits or life style. It's my life and I will live it as I please." Ask yourself the question, "Who pays for ill-chosen habits and life styles?" The price is paid personally, by parents and, ultimately, by tax payers. Statistics reveal how many tax dollars are spent for those who say, "It's none of your business." We need to remember what God's Word says, *"Fools, because of their transgression, and because of their iniquities, were afflicted."* That's the down and dark side, but verse 19 brings hope to the hopeless and a remedy for turning one's life around to experience how beautiful life can be. When a cry is made to God for help, He saves. *"He sent His word and healed them, and delivered them from their destructions." "Oh, that men would give thanks to the Lord for His goodness, and for His wonderful works to the children of men!"*

D. Fourth example of Distress - Tossed in a Tempest (Verses 23-32)

Seamen are tossed and driven by the tempest and then brought safe to shore. These are the perils of the waters. It is God who raises the storm; it is God who stills it. Wise men of this world need look no farther than the physical laws by which God acts. The Holy Spirit, through the psalmist, gives us a picture of the awful conflict between the elements as the work of God. In our individual lives, storms come and, in the rage of the storm, it seems that God is indifferent to our situation. But He is awakened by our cry. He makes the storm to calm so that the waves are still and we may experience a sweet quietness.

In verses 33-42, the character of the psalm changes. Instead of examples of deliverance from peril and thanksgiving for God's mercies, we have instances of God's providential government of the world given in two series of contrasts. Verses 33-39 tell of God's changing the productiveness of the land because of the character of those who inhabited it. The fruitful, well-watered land of the wicked was smitten like the rich plain of Sodom. It became desolate and changed into a salt-marsh. Immediately after, the wilderness of the hungry was blessed with water and made fertile to produce corn and wine. Verses 40 and 41 tells how the poor and humble are successful and the rich and the proud are overthrown. What is to be learned here is that God has such absolute control over the realm of nature that He can utterly reverse our circumstances. All is in His hands. Men work when God works. His blessing encourages the sower, cheers the planter and rewards the laborer. In the New Testament, we have the order: Paul planted, Apollos watered, and God gave the increase.

Knowledge is gained by observation, and with wonder and love, we see God's hand in our daily walk. God's providential dealing with us is, to a certain extent, influenced by our conduct. It is especially influenced by active, prayerful confidence in Him. It is by general laws that the providence of God directs the course of the world. The Legislator, like His laws, is always present in the world. Unlike the material world, God created us as free moral agents. God, as the God of providence, is also the God of grace. He is the God of grace that His providence may be the blessedness of mankind. He is the God of providence that His grace may be appropriated for eternal life.

III. Psalm 108

With slight variation, verses 1-5 of this psalm match Psalm 57:7-11 and verses 6-13 match Psalm 60:5-12. The commentary on these two Psalms is in Lesson #15. It is believed that David himself combined these passages to be the basis of a trilogy which includes Psalm 108 to Psalm 110.

IV. Psalm 109

This psalm consists of three parts:

1. Verses 1-5: A complaint of slanderous and malignant enemies.

2. Verses 6-20: A prayer for the punishment of the enemy.

3. Verses 21-31: A prayer for the sufferer's own deliverance and a promise of thanksgiving.

This psalm was written by King David. There are varying opinions about the application of this psalm. Some believe is was written when his enemies were trying to usurp his throne. Some believe it is applicable to the nation of Israel and its suffering from enemy nations, and applicable to the sufferings of Jesus Christ, the treachery of Judas and his miserable fate.

The writer speaks of being falsely accused and living in fear of death. The prayer for the punishment of the enemy is that the enemy meet the fate he has plotted for the innocent. Before this prayer of request for punishment, we read that the innocent had prayed for and tried to intercede for good on behalf of the wicked enemy. The enemy, who exuded corruption and destruction from his bones, would not be deterred from his evil path.

Today, we think about those who plot the destruction of the innocent by drugs, pornography and sexual child abuse. There are those who plot for the destruction of the values and life styles which are the foundations of a Christian society. We need to pray for those who do not know Christ as their personal Savior. There is a time, however, when those who refuse to listen to the gospel of Jesus Christ, refuse to repent of their sins and continue to inflict corruption and destruction, will experience God's judgment.

Just as David ended this psalm with praise and thanksgiving, we need to remember to express our thankfulness to God for His mercies upon us.

V. Psalm 110

The words of Christ, in Matthew 22:41-46; Mark 12:35-37; and Luke 20:41-44, would help us to know that this psalm is a direct prophecy of Himself. According to these words, there is no reference here to David or to any king of Israel as a type of Christ. This psalm is a counterpart to Psalm 2. It is clearly Messianic; it is quoted or referred to seven times in the New Testament. This psalm is not like other Messianic psalms, typical, but is directly prophetic of

Messiah, and of Him only. The following paragraphs are a paraphrase of the psalm attributed to J. J. Steward Perowne from his book on the Psalms.

(Verse 1) "Thus saith Jehovah—it is His revelation that I hear; it is His Word addressed to One who, though He be My Son, is yet my Lord—'I give Thee honor and dignity equal to my own, I associate Thee with Myself kingly rule and dominion, until I have subdued every enemy who shall dare to lift himself against Thee.'"

(Verses 2-3) Then turning to the King who has thus been solemnly placed on the throne of Jehovah, and who rules as His viceregent (a person appointed to perform functions of a king) in Zion, the psalmist says: "From Zion, Thy royal seat, shall Jehovah Himself, on whose throne Thou sittest, stretch out the sceptre of Thy dominion. So close shall be the fellowship between Him and Thee. Thou shalt sit on His throne: He shall wield Thy sceptre; His might shall be Thy might, His kingdom shall be Thy kingdom, and Thou shalt not only subdue Thine enemies, but before they are vanquished Thou shalt rule in the midst of them. When Thou goest forth to war, Thine own people shall flock with glad and willing hearts to Thy standard. They shall come clad, not in armor, but in holy vestments as ministering priests, for Thou hast consecrated them to be Thy priestly soldiers. They shall come a youthful host, in numbers numberless as the dew, bright and fresh as the dew from the womb of the morning."

(Verse 4) "Yet another solemn word concerning Thee have I heard. It is a word confirmed by an oath, the oath of the Most High, which cannot be broken. By that oath He hath made Thee Priest as well as King; King Thou art, Priest Thou shalt be henceforth. Priest not after the law of carnal commandment, or by descent through the Levitical priesthood, but after the order of Melchizedek; Priest, therefore, not of the Jew only, but of the Gentile also; Priest not for a time, but forever."

(Verse 5-7) Then, looking on the leader, the host, the conflict, the poet exclaims "'The Lord, the God of hosts who is with Thee, O King, who is at Thy right hand to succor and give Thee the victory in the battle, hath already crushed the rival monarchs

that dispute Thy sway. Thou shalt be a judge and ruler among nations whom He has given Thee as thine inheritance. The vast battlefield is strewn with corpses of Thy foes. Far and wide Thou hast extended Thy conquests vanquishing one leader after another, and Thou shalt reap the fruit of Thy victories, like a warrior who, pressing hotly on the rear of his enemies as they flee before him, scarcely pause for a moment to snatch a hasty draught from the wayside brook, and then with renewed ardor, with head erect and kindling eye, continues the pursuit. Thus shall victory be crowned, and not a foe remain.'"

This psalm completes the prophetic picture of the conquering Messiah. *"Sit at My right hand"* is equivalent to saying, "Be thou associated with Me in my kingly dignity, in My power and universal dominion."

Daniel 7:13-14 also refers to the conquering Messiah, *". . .one like the Son of Man, coming with the clouds of heaven! He came to the Ancient of Days, . . .then to Him was given dominion and glory and a kingdom, that all peoples, nations, and languages should serve Him."*

Two passages, one from the Psalms and the other from Daniel, were combined by our Lord Himself when standing before the high-priest. He said, *"hereafter you will see the Son of Man sitting at the right hand of the Power, and coming on the clouds of heaven."* (Matthew 26:64). In Acts 2:34-36, we read that the same interpretation was given by Peter. The right hand is a symbol of power. Therefore a seat at the right hand of a king implies a participation in His power. Assigned to the Messiah is the special and extraordinary power of total subjugation of His enemies. The idea throughout Psalm 110 is that it is in and through Messiah that the Lord acts for the destruction of His enemies. The rod of the Lord's strength was to be sent forth *"out of Zion."* It is the Gospel which is to subdue the world to Christ. It would first go forth into the world from Jerusalem where the hill of Zion stood. Other prophecies indicate the same. Isaiah said, *"Out of Zion shall go forth the law"* (the new law of grace which is to convert the Gentiles) *"and the Word of the Lord from Jerusalem"* (Isaiah 2:3). The prophet Zechariah said, *"It shall be that living waters shall flow from Jerusalem"* (Zechariah 14:8).

God, who holds the sceptre of His anointed and assures Him of victory, has also given Him a willing people working in their hearts by His Spirit.

In verse four, reference is made to Melchisedec. In Hebrews 7:15-17 we read, *"And it is yet far more evident if, in the likeness of Melchizedek, there arises another priest who has come, not according to the law of a fleshly commandment, but according to the power of an endless life. For He testifies: 'You are a priest forever According to the order of Melchizedek.'"* The priesthood of Melchisedec was a divinely instituted prophetic figure or type of the priesthood of Christ, especially in its combination with His royal dominion. He is not descended from Levi, but from Judah, and is a King on the throne of David; yet He is a Priest, a High Priest in the temple of God. Zechariah 6:12-13 says *"Then speak to him, saying, 'Thus says the Lord of hosts, saying: "Behold, the Man whose name is the BRANCH! From His place He shall branch out, and He shall build the temple of the Lord; Yes, He shall build the temple of the Lord. He shall bear the glory, and shall sit and rule on His throne; so He shall be a priest on His throne, and the counsel of peace shall be between them both."* The Jews questioned whether Christ, a descendant of Judah rather than of Levi, could be a priest. Melchisedec's name, parentage, birth, and death were not to be found in any priestly genealogy. He owed his position to direct divine appointment on personal grounds, and not to descent from an hereditary line. He had no successor in his priesthood, but held it until the object of his appointment was accomplished. The writer proves in this and other ways, not only that Christ was truly a priest, but that His priesthood was superior to that of Aaron.

VI. Psalms 111 and 112

These two psalms are referred to as alphabetical psalms. In both, the letters of the Hebrew alphabet mark not only the beginning verses, as in other psalms, but the beginning of each several clauses of the verses. In both, there are exactly twenty-two lines with each line consisting usually of three words. In both, the order of the alphabet is strictly preserved. In Psalm 111, the mighty deeds, the glory and the righteousness of God are celebrated in the assembly of the upright. In Psalm 112, the righteousness, the goodness and

the blessedness of the upright themselves is described and expanded. The one sets forth God, His work and His attributes; the other describes the work and character of those who fear and honor God. In Psalm 111:3, it is said of the Lord that *"His righteousness endures forever."* In Psalm 112:3, the same thing is said of the person who fears God. In Psalm 111:4, it says of the Lord that "He is gracious and of tender compassion." In Psalm 112:4, the same characteristic is given of the upright. In Psalm 111, the faithfulness of the Lord to His Covenant is prominent (verse 5, and 9) and in the 112th Psalm, the faithfulness of the righteous man, his trust in God, is prominent (verses 7, 8).

A. Psalm 111

The Psalmist declared, *"I will praise the Lord with my whole heart, in the assembly of the upright and in the congregation."* He had resolved to worship God both personally and in public. The reason for worship is given in verses 2 and 3: *"The works of the Lord are great, studied by all who have pleasure in them. His work is honorable and glorious, and His righteousness endures forever."* The greatness of His works is manifest equally in immensity and variety. He gives to every plant its leaf and flower and fruit. He gives to every animal its faculties and functions. To every person, He gives understanding, affections, and will. The magnitude of His works is beyond human comprehension. How often do we take time to consider and worship Him for His wonderful gifts? We need to make it a priority to see and admire, to reverence, to love and delight in God who has abundantly blessed us through His works. The Christian scholar will find inexhaustible subjects for study and contemplation in His wonderful works.

Verses 5-9 tell of God's goodness in supplying the needs of His people. He gave them manna in the wilderness. He provided for their needs in Canaan. He kept His covenant which He made to their fathers. He gave them their promised inheritance. His commandments are as His covenant, dependable and sure. The great seal of all is the redemption which He accomplished for His people. He who brought them out of Egypt will never permit His covenant to fail. Verse 9 says, *"holy and awesome is His name."* God's name is never to be used in a careless manner. Whether we pray or praise, we must be deeply possessed with a sense of His excellency. Verse 10 brings us to a conclusion of the psalm. Since God's commandments are as His covenant, dependable and sure, the first step towards wisdom is reverence for God. Reverence is proven by obedience to His will. Those who live according to His will and His commandments live wisely.

B. Psalm 112

The preceding psalm, Psalm 111, ends with, *"The fear of the Lord is the beginning of wisdom; a good understanding have all those who do His commandments. His praise endures forever."* Psalm 112 begins with *"Blessed is the man who fears the Lord, who delights greatly in His commandments."* The fear spoken of in these psalms is an awe, a reverence of love, that looks up and experiences no deeper joy than to be near the Lord. This brings an inseparable bond that trusts, that loves and submits. The psalmist gives praise to God for the blessings He bestows upon those who wisely fear Him and keep His commandments. Those who are wise are blessed in their children and their children's children. *"Wealth and riches will be in his house, and his righteousness endures forever."* The wealth in his house is made sure under the economy of his integrity and righteousness. Righteousness has its roots in the righteousness of God. It is not a striving to copy God. It is God's gift and God's work. Another blessing: *"Unto the upright there arises light in the darkness."* " While we are on earth, we are subject to a threefold darkness: the darkness of error, the darkness of sorrow, and the darkness of death. To dispel these, God visits us by His Word with a threefold 'light': the light of truth, the light of comfort, and the light of life" (G. Horne). The words "gracious and full of compassion, and righteous" are generally applied to God, but in this text, they refer to "the upright". Having experienced the graciousness, compassion and righteousness of God the Father, the children of God seek to be gracious, full of compassion and righteous toward others.

Verse five says, *"A good man deals graciously and lends; he will guide his affairs with discretion."* There are many less fortunate people in the world than ourselves and God calls on us to share our blessings with others. God is giving all the time. God blesses us for giving. We are to be stewards of that which God has blessed us with. We need to prayerfully and carefully make sure that our giving is done in such a manner as to bring glory to His name. Many, the world over, are suffering from lack of the bare necessities of existence. All we have belongs to God. He has given us the wisdom, knowledge and good health which has enabled us to be successful. These are God's blessings to us. Giving that others might hear the gospel, visiting the sick and the prisoner, helping the poor and helpless, caring for the fatherless and widow are concerns we should share as Christians. God has blessed us materially and with the privilege of studying His word. We are to be the means through which others can come to know Jesus Christ and share in the blessing of eternal life.

VII.   Psalms 113 - 118

This group of psalms is called the praise psalms. Matthew 26:30 and Mark 14:26 makes reference to them. They were sung at the family celebration of the passover. Psalms 113 and 114 were sung before the emptying of the second cup before the meal. Psalms 115 to 118 were sung after the meal and after the filling of the fourth cup. In all probability, our Lord and His apostles sang Psalms 115-118 after the passover and just before they left the upper room.

The Jewish tradition of singing these six psalms at the family celebration of the Passover is an indication of how they are linked in subject. They all sing of God the Redeemer, and relate some aspect of His redeeming character. We can see how poignant these psalms would be in the life of the Redeemer while celebrating the passover feast with His disciples in the upper room.

A. Psalm 113

This first psalm in the series of praise psalms was sung both before the meal at Passover and in the temple as part of the temple worship service. Even though it has been almost 2,000 years since the destruction of the temple, this psalm is still recited in Israel eighteen times a year.

B. Psalm 114

This psalm is considered the most beautiful of all the psalms which touch on the early history of Israel. In reflecting on the Israelites' journey from

Egypt to the promised land, the Psalmist inquired of the sea why it parted for Israel to walk through as on dry land, the rushing Jordan why it stopped in its course and the cliffs of Sinai why they shook to their base. The psalmist then answered for them with a triumphant exclamation. All nature trembles in the presence of God!

The psalmist's questioning was the means by which he gave all the opportunity to consider the power behind such miraculous events. Had the name of God appeared earlier in the psalm, there could be no wonder why the mountains should leap and the sea be driven back. Every time the psalm is read or sung, we should be moved in awe at the power and majesty of our God.

C. Psalm 115

This psalm was probably written for the service of the second temple. The mockery of their heathen adversaries was still fresh in the minds of the returned exiles and contempt for the idolatries which they had witnessed in Babylon was still fresh in their hearts. The psalm opens with a confession of unworthiness and a prayer that God would vindicate His own honor against the mockery of the heathen. In verse 3, God is exalted as the invisible, omnipotent, Supreme Ruler of the universe. In verses 4-8, the psalmist speaks with contempt of the helplessness of idols and the folly of their worshippers. In verses 9-11, all in Israel, the priests and people, are admonished to put their trust in God alone. God alone is worthy of trust. He alone is the help and shield of His people. In verses 12-18, the Psalm promises that God will give His blessing to them that trust in Him. The psalmist concluded with, *"Praise the Lord."*

D. Psalm 116

"I love the Lord" (verse 1). The true love of God is the love of His truth, of His holiness and of His will. True love is that which reflects itself in obedience. The psalmist's expression of love to God flowed from a heart grateful for the mercies experienced. After the expression of love, he reviewed God's goodness to all. The psalmist then promised that he would confess how great a debt of love he owed to God and committed himself to His service before the assembled congregation. This psalm gives insight into the depth of the religious life of individuals after their return from exile. Much of the psalm reminds us of earlier psalms and especially the psalms of David.

E. Psalm 117

This is the shortest of all the psalms. It is an exhortation to all the nations to glorify the Lord. The nations could not be expected to join in praise to God unless they also were partakers of the benefits enjoyed by Israel. Throughout the Old Testament, the scriptures give evidence that the grace and mercy of Israel's God was not to be confined to one nation, but was for all.

F. Psalm 118

Martin Luther's comment on Psalm 118 was, "This is my psalm, my chosen psalm. I love them all; I love all Holy Scripture, which is my consolation and my life. But this psalm is nearest my heart, and I have a peculiar right to call it mine. It has saved me from many a pressing danger, from which no emperor, nor kings, nor sages, nor saints could have saved me. I am not jealous of my property; I would divide it with the whole world. And would to God that all men would claim the psalm as especially theirs! It would be the most touching quarrel, the most agreeable to God, a quarrel of union and perfect charity" (Luther).

The speaker throughout Psalm 118 is Israel, God's chosen people. The deliverance celebrated is no doubt the deliverance from exile in Babylon. The psalm was designed to be sung in the temple worship. It has two divisions:

1. Verses 1-19: Sung by the procession. The procession was led by the priests and Levites who went to the temple with sacrificial animals. With verse 19, the procession would be at the entrance of the temple.

2. Verses 20-27: Sung by the Levites who received the festive procession. Verse 28 gives the answer to the Levites by those in the procession, and verse 29 was the concluding song sung by all assembled.

Daily Bible Study Questions for Group Discussion

Note: Read notes and Scripture references before answering the questions. Some questions are for those more advanced in Bible Study. Try to answer all questions but don't be discouraged if some seem a little hard. Unless otherwise instructed, use Bible only in answering questions.

FIRST DAY: Read notes on lesson 21.

    1. What was most meaningful to you in the notes?

    2. What was most meaningful to you from the lecture?

    3. Which would you choose from this lesson as your favorite psalm or verse and why?

SECOND DAY: Read Psalm 119:1-48.

    4. **Read verses 1-24.**
        a) How many times is "heart" used in this chapter?

        b) Two verses mention reasons for people being blessed. Give the verses and reasons for their being blessed.

    5. **Read verses 25-32.** The psalmist indicated he had to make a choice. What was he choosing between?

6. **Read verses 33-48**.
   a) What two things in particular does the psalmist desire to be kept from?

   b) What two parts of our body do these involve?

THIRD DAY: Read Psalm 119:49-96.

7. From **verses 49-64**, what verb is mentioned three times in reference to what we should do with God's Word?

8. **Read verses 49 -72.**
   a) In which three verses does the psalmist speak of suffering affliction?

   b) What was the source of comfort in his affliction?

9. **Text work sheet (verses 73-96)**
   What did the psalmist pray for? Why? Underline each answer with a different color pencil.

10. **Read verses 89-91.** What is a common characteristic of both God's words and His works?

FOURTH DAY: Read Psalm 119:97-120.

11. From the psalmist's experience, how do **verses 97-104** illustrate that obedience is essential to understanding and appreciating the truth of God?

12. a) In considering **verses 105 to 112**, do you think the psalmist could have been persecuted because of his devotion to God's Word?

    b) Is this a problem today when you take a Biblical position on social issues and also on holy living?

13. In **Verses 113-120**, what did the psalmist say God was to him?

FIFTH DAY: Read Psalm 119:121-144.

14. What evidence is given in these verses that indicate the psalmist was subjected to opposition?

15. Underline on your text work sheet the different phrases that are explicit prayers.

16. How does the psalmist describe God's Word in **Verses 121-144**?

SIXTH DAY: Read Psalm 119:145-176.

17. **Read verses 145-160.**
    a) Four times in these verses, the psalmist prays for the same thing from the Lord. In what verses is the prayer found?

    b) To pray and study God's word involves time. What times did the psalmist set aside for prayer and communion with God?

18. From **verses 161 to 168**, give at least three characteristics of the psalmist's heart attitude towards the Word of God.

19. Knowledge of the Word led to a life of praise for the psalmist. From **verses 161-176**, list the verses that indicate his praise.

Psalm 119

1 Blessed are the undefiled in the way, Who walk in the law of the LORD!

2 Blessed are those who keep His testimonies, Who seek Him with the whole heart!

3 They also do no iniquity; They walk in His ways.

4 You have commanded us To keep Your precepts diligently.

5 Oh, that my ways were directed To keep Your statutes!

6 Then I would not be ashamed, When I look into all Your commandments.

7 I will praise You with uprightness of heart, When I learn Your righteous judgments.

8 I will keep Your statutes; Oh, do not forsake me utterly!

9 How can a young man cleanse his way? By taking heed according to Your word.

10 With my whole heart I have sought You; Oh, let me not wander from Your commandments!

11 Your word I have hidden in my heart, That I might not sin against You!

12 Blessed are You, O LORD! Teach me Your statutes!

13 With my lips I have declared All the judgments of Your mouth.

14 I have rejoiced in the way of Your testimonies, As much as in all riches.

15 I will meditate on Your precepts, And contemplate Your ways.

16 I will delight myself in Your statutes; I will not forget Your word.

17 Deal bountifully with Your servant, That I may live and keep Your word.

18 Open my eyes, that I may see Wondrous things from Your law.

19 I am a stranger in the earth; Do not hide Your commandments from me.

20 My soul breaks with longing For Your judgments at all times.

21 You rebuke the proud; the cursed, Who stray from Your commandments.

22 Remove from me reproach and contempt, For I have kept Your testimonies.

23 Princes also sit and speak against me, But Your servant meditates on Your statutes.

24 Your testimonies also are my delight And my counselors.

25 My soul clings to the dust; Revive me according to Your word.

26 I have declared my ways, and You answered me; Teach me Your statutes.

27 Make me understand the way of Your precepts; So shall I meditate on Your wondrous works.

28 My soul melts from heaviness; Strengthen me according to Your word.

29 Remove from me the way of lying, And grant me Your law graciously.

30 I have chosen the way of truth; Your judgments I have laid before me.

31 I cling to Your testimonies; O LORD, do not put me to shame!

32 I will run the course of Your commandments, For You shall enlarge my heart.

33 Teach me, O LORD, the way of Your statutes, And I shall keep it to the end.

34 Give me understanding, and I shall keep Your law; Indeed, I shall observe it with my whole heart.

35 Make me walk in the path of Your commandments, For I delight in it.

36 Incline my heart to Your testimonies, And not to covetousness.

37 Turn away my eyes from looking at worthless things, And revive me in Your way.

38 Establish Your word to Your servant, Who is devoted to fearing You.

39 Turn away my reproach which I dread, For Your judgments are good.

40 Behold, I long for Your precepts; Revive me in Your righteousness.

41 Let Your mercies come also to me, O LORD; Your salvation according to Your word.

42 So shall I have an answer for him who reproaches me, For I trust in Your word.

43 And take not the word of truth utterly out of my mouth, For I have hoped in Your ordinances.

44 So shall I keep Your law continually, Forever and ever.

45 And I will walk at liberty, For I seek Your precepts.

46 I will speak of Your testimonies also before kings, And will not be ashamed.

47 And I will delight myself in Your commandments, Which I love.

48 My hands also I will lift up to Your commandments, Which I love, And I will meditate on Your statutes.

49 Remember the word to Your servant, Upon which You have caused me to hope.

50 This is my comfort in my affliction, For Your word has given me life.

51 The proud have me in great derision, Yet I do not turn aside from Your law.

52 I remembered Your judgments of old, O LORD, And have comforted myself.

53 Indignation has taken hold of me Because of the wicked, who forsake Your law.

54 Your statutes have been my songs In the house of my pilgrimage.

55 I remember Your name in the night, O LORD, And I keep Your law.

56 This has become mine, Because I kept Your precepts.

57 You are my portion, O LORD; I have said that I would keep Your words.

58 I entreated Your favor with my whole heart; Be merciful to me according to Your word.

59 I thought about my ways, And turned my feet to Your testimonies.

60 I made haste, and did not delay To keep Your commandments.

61 The cords of the wicked have bound me, But I have not forgotten Your law.

62 At midnight I will rise to give thanks to You, Because of Your righteous judgments.

63 I am a companion of all who fear You, And of those who keep Your precepts.

64 The earth, O LORD, is full of Your mercy; Teach me Your statutes.

65 You have dealt well with Your servant, O LORD, according to Your word.

66 Teach me good judgment and knowledge, For I believe Your commandments.

67 Before I was afflicted I went astray, But now I keep Your word.

68 You are good, and do good; Teach me Your statutes.

69 The proud have forged a lie against me, But I will keep Your precepts with my whole heart.

70 Their heart is as fat as grease, But I delight in Your law.

71 It is good for me that I have been afflicted, That I may learn Your statutes.

72 The law of Your mouth is better to me Than thousands of coins of gold and silver.

73 Your hands have made me and fashioned me; Give me understanding, that I may learn Your commandments.

74 Those who fear You will be glad when they see me, Because I have hoped in Your word.

75 I know, O LORD, that Your judgments are right, And that in faithfulness You have afflicted me.

76 Let, I pray, Your merciful kindness be for my comfort, According to Your word to Your servant.

77 Let Your tender mercies come to me, that I may live; For Your law is my delight.

78 Let the proud be ashamed, For they treated me wrongfully with falsehood; But I will meditate on Your precepts. 79 Let those who fear You turn to me, Those who know Your testimonies.

80 Let my heart be blameless regarding Your statutes, That I may not be ashamed.

81 My soul faints for Your salvation, But I hope in Your word.

82 My eyes fail from searching Your word, Saying, "When will You comfort me?"

83 For I have become like a wineskin in smoke, Yet I do not forget Your statutes.

84 How many are the days of Your servant? When will You execute judgment on those who persecute me?

85 The proud have dug pits for me, Which is not according to Your law.

86 All Your commandments are faithful; They persecute me wrongfully; Help me!

87 They almost made an end of me on earth, But I did not forsake Your precepts.

88 Revive me according to Your lovingkindness, So that I may keep the testimony of Your mouth.

89 Forever, O LORD, Your word is settled in heaven.

90 Your faithfulness endures to all generations; You established the earth, and it abides.

91 They continue this day according to Your ordinances, For all are Your servants.

92 Unless Your law had been my delight, I would then have perished in my affliction.

93 I will never forget Your precepts, For by them You have given me life.

94 I am Yours, save me; For I have sought Your precepts.

95 The wicked wait for me to destroy me, But I will consider Your testimonies.

96 I have seen the consummation of all perfection, But Your commandment is exceedingly broad.

97 Oh, how I love Your law! It is my meditation all the day.

98 You, through Your commandments, make me wiser than my enemies; For they are ever with me.

99 I have more understanding than all my teachers, For Your testimonies are my meditation.

100 I understand more than the ancients, Because I keep Your precepts.

101 I have restrained my feet from every evil way, That I may keep Your word.

102 I have not departed from Your judgments, For You Yourself have taught me.

103 How sweet are Your words to my taste, Sweeter than honey to my mouth!

104 Through Your precepts I get understanding; Therefore I hate every false way.

105 Your word is a lamp to my feet And a light to my path.

106 I have sworn and confirmed That I will keep Your righteous judgments.

107 I am afflicted very much; Revive me, O LORD, according to Your word.

108 Accept, I pray, the freewill offerings of my mouth, O LORD, And teach me Your judgments.

109 My life is continually in my hand, Yet I do not forget Your law.

110 The wicked have laid a snare for me, Yet I have not strayed from Your precepts.

111 Your testimonies I have taken as a heritage forever, For they are the rejoicing of my heart.

112 I have inclined my heart to perform Your statutes Forever, to the very end.

113 I hate the double-minded, But I love Your law.

114 You are my hiding place and my shield; I hope in Your word.

115 Depart from me, you evildoers, For I will keep the commandments of my God!

116 Uphold me according to Your word, that I may live; And do not let me be ashamed of my hope.

117 Hold me up, and I shall be safe, And I shall observe Your statutes continually.

118 You reject all those who stray from Your statutes, For their deceit is falsehood.

119 You put away all the wicked of the earth like dross; Therefore I love Your testimonies.

120 My flesh trembles for fear of You, And I am afraid of Your judgments.

121 I have done justice and righteousness; Do not leave me to my oppressors.

122 Be surety for Your servant for good; Do not let the proud oppress me.

123 My eyes fail from seeking Your salvation And Your righteous word.

124 Deal with Your servant according to Your mercy, And teach me Your statutes.

125 I am Your servant; Give me understanding, That I may know Your testimonies.

126 It is time for You to act, O LORD, For they have regarded Your law as void.

127 Therefore I love Your commandments More than gold, yes, than fine gold!

128 Therefore all Your precepts concerning all things I consider to be right; I hate every false way.

129 Your testimonies are wonderful; Therefore my soul keeps them.

130 The entrance of Your words gives light; It gives understanding to the simple.

131 I opened my mouth and panted, For I longed for Your commandments.

132 Look upon me and be merciful to me, As Your custom is toward those who love Your name.

133 Direct my steps by Your word, And let no iniquity have dominion over me.

134 Redeem me from the oppression of man, That I may keep Your precepts.

135 Make Your face shine upon Your servant, And teach me Your statutes.

136 Rivers of water run down from my eyes, Because men do not keep Your law.

137 Righteous are You, O LORD, And upright are Your judgments.

138 Your testimonies, which You have commanded, Are righteous and very faithful.

139 My zeal has consumed me, Because my enemies have forgotten Your words.

140 Your word is very pure; Therefore Your servant loves it.

141 I am small and despised, Yet I do not forget Your precepts.

142 Your righteousness is an everlasting righteousness, And Your law is truth.

143 Trouble and anguish have overtaken me, Yet Your commandments are my delights.

144 The righteousness of Your testimonies is everlasting; Give me understanding, and I shall live.

145 I cry out with my whole heart; Hear me, O LORD! I will keep Your statutes.

146 I cry out to You; Save me, and I will keep Your testimonies.

147 I rise before the dawning of the morning, And cry for help; I hope in Your word.

148 My eyes are awake through the night watches, That I may meditate on Your word.

149 Hear my voice according to Your lovingkindness; O LORD, revive me according to Your justice.

150 They draw near who follow after wickedness; They are far from Your law.

151 You are near, O LORD, And all Your commandments are truth.

152 Concerning Your testimonies, I have known of old that You have founded them forever.

153 Consider my affliction and deliver me, For I do not forget Your law.

154 Plead my cause and redeem me; Revive me according to Your word.

155 Salvation is far from the wicked, For they do not seek Your statutes.

156 Great are Your tender mercies, O LORD; Revive me according to Your judgments.

157 Many are my persecutors and my enemies, Yet I do not turn from Your testimonies.

158 I see the treacherous, and am disgusted, Because they do not keep Your word.

159 Consider how I love Your precepts; Revive me, O LORD, according to Your lovingkindness.

160 The entirety of Your word is truth, And every one of Your righteous judgments endures forever.

161 Princes persecute me without a cause, But my heart stands in awe of Your word.

162 I rejoice at Your word As one who finds great treasure.

163 I hate and abhor lying, But I love Your law.

164 Seven times a day I praise You, Because of Your righteous judgments.

165 Great peace have those who love Your law, And nothing causes them to stumble.

166 LORD, I hope for Your salvation, And I do Your commandments.

167 My soul keeps Your testimonies, And I love them exceedingly.

168 I keep Your precepts and Your testimonies, For all my ways are before You.

169 Let my cry come before You, O LORD; Give me understanding according to Your word.

170 Let my supplication come before You; Deliver me according to Your word.

171 My lips shall utter praise, For You teach me Your statutes.

172 My tongue shall speak of Your word, For all Your commandments are righteousness.

173 Let Your hand become my help, For I have chosen Your precepts.

174 I long for Your salvation, O LORD, And Your law is my delight.

175 Let my soul live, and it shall praise You; And let Your judgments help me.

176 I have gone astray like a lost sheep; Seek Your servant, For I do not forget Your commandments.

Notes

Notes

Psalm 119

I. Psalm 119 - Introduction

This psalm is a prolonged meditation upon the Word, its effects, and the strength and happiness it gives throughout one's life. One author commented that in the German translation of the Bible, this psalm was given the title: The Christian golden ABC of the praise, love, virtue, and usefulness of the Word of God. The psalmist's meditations were interspersed with prayers. His petition was for God's assistance in living life according to His Word. To be able to understand and enjoy this psalm, we must learn to love and practice the sacred Word. It is a touch stone for spiritual life to those who read it. The psalmist made known his design in the first verses of the psalm and pursued it to the end. Holiness is represented as the immediate object of a spiritual taste and delight. The psalmist referred to the content of Scripture as God's law, His way, His testimonies, His commandments, His precepts, His Word, His judgments, His righteousness, His statutes and His truth. All are His eternal truths.

A. Psalm 119:1-16

The psalmist began with a description of the way to blessedness in the same way Christ began His sermon on the Mount. The word blessed is found many times in the Book of Psalms. *"Blessed are the undefiled in the way."* They are blessed who are in the way. The "way" is the path which follows the law of the Lord.

The Word of God is called His testimony. It testifies of His will concerning His service and also of His favor and goodwill concerning His own in Christ Jesus. If God's Word were no more than a law, we as His creatures would be bound to obey it. However, it is also a testimony of His love. Faith involves both a belief in His promises and obedience to His Word. We cannot cut faith in half and exercise the one aspect without the other. Some people say that they delight in God's promises but choose to ignore His commandments. Whoever takes God at His word will take all His words. There is no faith without obedience; there is no obedience without faith.

"...and that seek Him with the whole heart." There is so much said about seeking pardon, seeking peace, and seeking acceptance with God that we are prone to believe these are the ultimate in the Christian life. The Bible only represents them as a means to an end. These blessings are just the beginning. They increase our desire and lead us to something higher and better. In them, we lay the foundation of the Christian life, but they are not life itself. The ultimate life is in God. It is only as we seek Him with a whole heart that we can truly enjoy life. God's commandments are exalted into privileges; the ordinances become means of fellowship with God. The believer draws near to God and God draws near to him in prayer, in praise, and in hearing the Word. In these, God manifests His gracious presence. God's grace is received with thankfulness and rejoicing. *"They also do no iniquity: they walk in His ways."* This refers to an attitude of the heart. We will not know perfection until we go to be with Christ. We are all "Christians under construction." Great care must be taken to build on a firm foundation, and Christ is our sure foundation. The master plan is found in His Word. The Christian experience is a growing experience. We must trust that the Holy Spirit will be our teacher and guide for each day. Through the infirmity of the flesh, the subtlety of Satan, and the allurements of the world, we are subjected to temptations. Iniquity or sinning generally involves three steps, (1) allowing temptation a place to take root, (2) a delight in committing the sin, and (3) continuing in it. *"You have commanded us to keep Your precepts diligently. Oh, that my ways were directed (or established) to keep Your statutes!"* (verses 4-5). In our inability to be perfect, we can only return the mandate to heaven with an earnest

prayer that the Lord would write upon our hearts those statutes to which He requires obedience. The beauty and glory of spiritual realities do not come all at once, but come in the course of Christian experience. Paul admonished that we should keep a good conscience in all things toward God and men. *"Then I would not be ashamed, when I look into all Your commandments."* (verse 6). The psalmist desired to learn the Word and will of God. Studying God's Word is vital to Christian living. We can't walk or live by something we don't know, therefore we must choose to read and study our guide book. Our choice to walk in the way, the way of God's Word, is a choice we make every day.

"How can a young man cleanse his way? **By taking** heed according to Your word" (Verse 9).

The youth of today will determine the future of our society. *"The fear of the Lord is the beginning of wisdom"* (Psalm 111:10). As adults, we must not neglect the explicit instruction to train and teach our children God's laws and ways. They need to know by precept and example what God expects and what His Word teaches. Their primary instructor is the parent. Parental teaching is augmented by the church. Based on the Biblical teaching of the parents and the church, young people themselves must "take heed" according to that word. Choices always have consequences. The friends they choose and the places they go all have an influence on their lives. Our influence through the Word and daily prayer for them must begin at a very early age and continue as they mature into adulthood. As with all other responsibilities, our children become increasingly responsible to make right choices in living according to God's Word. We are responsible to teach them, to train them and to pray for them. They have the responsibility to "take heed."

Memorizing scripture is also very important. *"Your word I have hidden in my heart, that I might not sin against You!"* (verse 11). Put God's Word into memory where it will be ever present and ready to guide the affections and purposes of our lives. Every day should include a time for prayer and meditation on the Word of God. Parents should share a time of devotion with their children. There is a great tendency for Christians to excuse themselves from this duty because they are too busy. As a consequence, lives are lived at the starvation level. We become spiritually lean and barren because we do not feed on the Word. Joshua 1:8 says, *"This Book of the Law shall not depart from your mouth, but you shall meditate in it day and night, that you may **observe** to **do** according to all that is written in it."* Delight prevents forgetfulness for we remember that which the heart delights in.

B. Psalm 119:17-32

Remembering our weaknesses, emptiness and helplessness, it is appropriate to pray, *"Lord, deal bountifully with thy servant."* The psalmist's request was not for a life of prosperity, but that he would keep God's word; that his eyes would be opened so that his heart would understand God's law. This prayer implies the Divine inspiration and authority of the Bible. The psalmist wanted to know God's Word well. What we need today is a more intense study of the Bible accompanied by the prayer of the psalmist.

Christians are but pilgrims traveling through this earthly life to heaven. The Bible is our guide book and map. It gives instructions for the journey and all the requirements for the traveler. Although the traveler may encounter rough roads and construction hazards, the word is a comfort and guide. It also prepares us for the end of the earthly journey. Heaven is the Christian's destination. Our inheritance, our kindred, our Saviour, our hope and our home is there. As we journey, God will hide neither His commandments nor Himself from those who prayerfully trust Him. When we reach our destination, we will be neither stranger nor pilgrim. The psalmist's cherished desire was for God's Word at all times. In the Word, He found answers for the necessities as well as for the joy of life.

From verses 21-24, opposition to God's word is evident. **Pride** makes people believe that they know better than God. **Reproach and contempt** came to the Psalmist from those who disdained God's Word. Few things are more difficult to tolerate than scorn. Young people often hide their faith for fear of scorn. The psalmist prayed that God would remove the reproach and contempt of those in positions of power that spoke against him. He gave us his method for withstanding those abuses: he meditated in God's statutes. They who make the Word their delight will always find it their counselor.

There is no sin that God abhors more than pride. It is a destructive principle that robs a Christian of sincerity and happiness. Pride is always active and subtle. Satan tries to mix its influence with every aspect of life so that an individual is unaware of it. Christians should be aware that they are not always cognizant of its subtle approach and therefore susceptible to this temptation.

The psalmist's complaint, in verse 25, is more an expression of conflict and humiliation than of despondency. His prayer to God was for quickening. This cry for quickening grace was the exercise of faith. Faith is the hand that takes hold of the promise, *"Revive me according to Your word."* occurs nine times and is found only in this psalm. It expresses the spiritual change by which we become a child of God. The source of spiritual change is the loving **Father**, redeeming **Son** and sanctifying **Spirit** (John 5:21; 6:63). The instrument by which it is effected is the Word.

"My soul melts from heaviness. . ." (verse 28). Heaviness makes a man stoop but a good word makes it glad. The psalmist's body was weary with sorrow, but God's Word strengthened him and lightened his load. The resources of God are inexhaustible and as Christians, God is our resource.

C. Psalm 119:29-48

In verses 33 to 36, there are four petitions: *"Teach me. . . Give me understanding. . . make me walk in the path of Your commandments, for I delight in it."* Luther translated these opening words as: "Point out to me," "Explain to me," "Lead me," and "Incline my heart." *"Turn away my eyes from looking at worthless things"* (verse 37). We must avoid whatever leads to sin. Sin can first enter the mind by the eye, and it is used by Satan as a gate for allurements. The prayer is not for the eyes to be shut, but "turned away", turned to the right objects. The love of the world is deterred only by the love of the Father. The most effective way of avoiding temptation is to be **revived** in God's way. This leaves no desire for beholding vanity and that which is forbidden in God's Word. Prayer is the preserving power of life to keep us from the evils which surround us. The psalmist prayed for the Lord to open his eyes to the wondrous things of the law. He prayed that the Lord

would teach him His statutes, remove from him the way of lying and turn his eyes away from beholding vanity. He also prayed that he would not fall prey to covetousness and that His heart would be inclined unto His commandments. He asked for teaching, direction and understanding. He asked for strength to avoid that which was evil. Each petition shows that the psalmist was aware of his need and of his complete dependence upon God.

In verses 45 to 48, we read: *"I will **walk** at liberty,"* *"I will **speak** of Your testimonies,"* *"I will **delight** myself in Your Commandments,"* and *I will **meditate** in Your statutes."* Discipleship is a loyal, constant following the Lord in obedience to His Word. This is not easy from a human point of view. It takes personal discipline, perseverance and determination. Each day we are subjected to choices. With God's help, a deep and devoted love for Jesus Christ, and the power of the Holy Spirit working in and through us, we will know that God has been in control of each day. There are bad days and good days. Thank God for His presence and help in both. The knowledge of God's Word dispels error. By showing the evil and dangers of sin, God's Word delivers us from sin's bondage and power. Sin is a hard taskmaster. Yielding to its pleasures begets paying its penalties. Christ alone can free us from such bondage. As we give our lives to Jesus Christ and obey His commandments, we will experience a freedom otherwise unknown (verse 45). In verses 46-48, the psalmist promised a threefold duty of thankfulness: **First**, the service of his tongue, and **second**, the service of his affections and **third**, the service of his actions. A good conscience always gives great consolation and an honest life gives us boldness to speak without fear or shame.

D. Psalm 119:49-64

"Remember the word to Your servant, upon which You have caused me to hope." Those who are God's servants have a right to the promises and may justly lay hold upon them. Those who obey God's precepts can rightly apply His promises to themselves. Make it clear that you are God's servant, and then these promises are your own — no less than if your name had been inserted in the promise and written in the Bible. Let us turn every promise into a prayer. God's promises are His bond. *"This is my comfort in my affliction, for Your word has given me life."*

The psalmist felt the reviving, restoring, life-giving power of the Word as he read and meditated. The believer has all God's unfailing promises to depend upon. As we depend, we gain strength through our own experiences of the faithfulness of God's Word. God's Word, received, loved and obeyed is the believer's true life. Love, faith and obedience bring communion with God. This is the life that triumphs over temptation; that sings in the hour of pain and death.

"I remembered Your judgments of old" (verse 52). The word "judgments" refers to God's righteous laws. The psalmist takes comfort in the fact that God's laws, the laws of His covenant, are ever true and ever in force. As God is unchanging and forever, so also are His statutes. The certainty of God's statutes is the rock upon which the psalmist can lean during times of hardships. *"Your statutes have been my songs"* (verse 54). God's statutes were the source of the psalmist's strength; the source of his songs. They gave him spiritual refreshing as he traveled through life here on earth and in all sets of circumstances.

Verse 56 says, *"This has become mine, because I kept Your precepts."* This comfort I enjoyed, this support in trouble, this confidence I was able to maintain *"because I kept Your precepts."* The psalmist did not say this I hoped for, but **"this I had."** We too can experience the comfort, the joy and strength that the psalmist experienced if we, like him, keep God's precepts.

God is all sufficient. If you have chosen Him as your "portion," you have God's infinite wisdom to direct you, His infinite knowledge to teach you, His infinite mercy to pity and save you, His infinite love to care and comfort you, and His infinite power to protect and keep you. *"I entreated Your favor."* *"I thought about my ways."* *"I made haste."* Entreat is to seek God's presence. If we would have favor and mercy from God, it must be on His terms. We must ask according to His will and according to His promises. The psalmist also said, "I thought." He meditated deeply. He considered the kind of life he had lived.

First, he pondered God's Word. Then he reflected on his own life. The result was a physical turning. He turned away from transgression and to the Word of God. Active obedience to God's Word and serious consideration about one's life result in a turning to God and living a new life. We call this conversion. Following his decision to turn to the Lord, the psalmist wasted no time — *"I made haste."* He was determined and so began to act. It is a serious matter to trifle with conviction. In a matter of eternal life and eternal death, the call is too clear for debate, and there is no time for delay. Today is God's time. Tomorrow ruins thousands. Resolutions, however sincere, and convictions however serious, *"will pass away as the morning cloud and as the early dew,"* unless they are carefully cherished. The more we defer, the more difficult and painful change will become. Satan is always there to bargain.

"At midnight I will rise to give thanks to You..." (verse 62). Some of us awaken in the night when something is troubling us and others of us just seem to have times of wakefulness in the night time. The psalmist spoke of his wise use of night time wakefulness. In the night his meditation was upon God and His statutes. If we spend the waking moments of the night with God, the darkness is not darkness with us, but *"the night shines as the day"* (Psalm 139:12). Midnight wakefulness would be sweeter than slumber, if we chose to count our blessings rather than our reasons for lack of sleep.

E. Psalm 119:65-80

Verse 65 is a summary of the psalmist's life. God has done all things well. God's benefits are tokens of His love bestowed on us according to His Word. The psalmist prayed for the knowledge of God's will. He took God's precepts upon trust, but then prayed that he would understand them. The sentiment of verse 67 has been echoed and its very words repeated by godly sufferers of every age. Affliction teaches us to live by faith and results in a closeness to God through prayer. There are many temptations today that seek to lure us from God: business, pleasure and prosperity. Sometimes God permits adversities and afflictions to bring us back in reconciliation with Him. Also we suffer afflictions because we live in an imperfect world. Our comfort is that God is always near to be our strength and our guide in every affliction, in every trouble. Let us draw near to Him, as the psalmist did, through the study of His Word and through prayer. Then we will come to know the strength and joy that only God can give in both the good times and the bad. It is characteristic of this psalm that the petition founded on the goodness of God's nature, on His mercy and on His infinite perfection is still *"teach me Your statutes"* (verse 68).

The craft and malice of his enemies caused the psalmist sorrow. But it did not create doubt about God's statutes and love. Instead, the malice of his enemies only led him to obey God with a more undivided heart (verse 69). We often learn more of God under the rod that strikes us than under the staff that comforts us (verse 71). Through the discipline of trial alone, men have been trained to thought and action, to endurance and achievement. The goodness of God to one becomes the joy and comfort of all (verse 74). The psalmist trusted fully in God's wisdom, God's power and God's love. *"I know, O Lord, that Your judgments are right, and that in faithfulness You have afflicted me."* He expressed a sure and happy confidence that all God had done, and would do, was right for him. The very words "I know" shows that this was a matter of faith, not of sight. God had shown Himself faithful. God deals with His children gently and lovingly.

The psalmist prayed that he would have God's "loving-kindness" and His "tender mercies" as his comfort in the midst of affliction. *"Let Your tender mercies come to me, that I may live; for Your law is my delight."* First, the psalmist sought mercy to forgive his sins; then he sought mercy to comfort him in his troubles. Then he sought mercy to live and not sin.

F. Psalm 119:81-96

"My soul faints for Your salvation, but I hope in Your word." The word "soul" refers to the psalmist's bones, his whole being. His whole body was bowed down waiting for God's salvation. Although he was tired at times with the afflictions experienced here on earth, he never doubted God's Word. He had a living faith in his heart. He believed the Word of grace and salvation and he hoped for the fulfillment of the promises of his Lord to be realized. He honored his Lord's Word, trusted in His faithfulness, and cast the anchor of his hope upon God's truth. Faith is not always able to understand God's promises with His providence, but we can still "hope" (trust) in God's Word. In Psalm 46:10, we are

admonished to *"Be still, and know that I am God."* Waiting time is a precious time and will not be lost time. God waits, not because He is reluctant to give, but that we may be ready to receive. *"When will You comfort me?"* Scriptures are given to us for guidance and for instruction. Comfort is a result of obedience to that instruction. *"Your Word is a lamp to my feet and a light to my path."* Our feet can be kept in the path of peace as we follow this light. Although the psalmist described his situation as a leather container or bottle shriveled in the smoke, he permitted nothing to deter him from God's Word. He felt that God's way might be rough, but it was right. Whatever God's commands might cost him personally, they were worth a commitment of faithfulness.

"Help me" — God help me. This is a prayer as precious as it is short. It suits a thousand conditions of need, pain, distress, weakness and sin. God's help is all sufficient. In verse 88, the quickening the Psalmist sought was the renewing day by day of the inner man. The source of this renewal is the loving kindness of God. Its effects are steadfast obedience to His will.

Verse 89 is the center of the psalm. In the first part, the psalmist spoke of his afflictions and life which are temporary. He spoke of his faith in God's statutes and their being a source of his renewal. In this second half we are given insight into the reason for his surety in God's statutes. *"The Lord's Word does not change: and in spite of all evil hindrances, the Lord will perfect concerning me the work that He has already begun."*

God's work of creation, the ordering of the seasons and the laws of nature upon which we can depend to send people into space, all speak to us of God's eternal wisdom and love. This world is the instrument by which God accomplishes His moral designs. The support of the Word is as sure as its basis. Martin Luther once said, "I have covenanted with my Lord, that He should not send me visions, or dreams, or even angels. I am content with this one gift of the Scriptures, which abundantly teaches and supplies all that is necessary both for this life and that which is to come."

G. Psalm 119:97-112

In these eight verses, as it is throughout the psalm, the law is spoken of as the Lord's. By histories, laws, prophecies, and promises, He wrote about Himself — the creator, preserver and deliver of mankind. The psalmist spoke of knowing, reading, hearing, speaking, and practicing the law. But he also spoke likewise of his love for the law. We may do all that is prescribed as to works and commandments of the law, and yet not love it. A love for God's law will cause us to study it and order our lives according to God's Word.

In verses 98-100, the psalmist referred to three classes of people: "enemies," "teachers" and "the aged." The enemies might excel in worldly wisdom, teachers might excel in their doctrine and the aged might excel in their counsel; yet, through the study of the Word of God, the psalmist had gained understanding which had made him wiser than them all. The Word of God is given for understanding and wisdom, to give us a light by which to live. *"Your word is a lamp to my feet and a light to my path"* (verse 105). Without this light, we all walk in darkness.

"Your testimonies I have taken as a heritage forever, for they are the rejoicing of my heart." (verse 111). Bible history is valuable. It gives us a rich variety of testimonies through the lives of His servants. When we think of Job, we think of patience. When we think of Abraham, we think of faith. When we think of Moses, we think of fidelity. When we think of Caleb, we think of brave hopefulness. When we think of Elijah, we think of zeal. When we think of Peter, we think of brash earnestness. This list could be continued with such people as: Samson, Samuel, Elisha, Ruth, Isaiah, Deborah, Paul, etc. The people of the Bible were individuals with unique personalities just as we are today. Through the reading of God's word, and through the lives of these people, we learn of God's laws and ways, His methods of teaching His people, of God's power, His purpose, His love and His hatred of sin. *"God, who at various times and in various ways spoke in time past to the fathers by the prophets, has in these last days spoken to us by His Son"* (Hebrews 1:1). For Abraham and Jacob, God's communication was direct. He communicated to others and communicates to us through the lessons of the Levitical code, the utterances of prophecy, the inspiration of the Psalms, the Gospel, the Epistles and the Apocalypse. The Bible is the book which brings unity to this mass of testimony. The testimony is of the Creator and preserver of heaven and earth.

H. Psalm 119:113-128

"You are my hiding place and my shield" (verse 114). This is complete security. God's people are safe under God's protection. Verse 117 is a prayer that God will hold us up and keep us safe from the dangers of a slippery path. Unfailing protection depends upon the upholding power of our faithful God.

If the wicked seem to prosper, remember it will not always be so. The wicked, full of lies and deceit, are often caught in their own snares. Even if it seems they are not, God's laws and judgment are sure (verse 118). Without a presiding authority, the whole universe would drift into anarchy. The Word of grace is made the Word of righteousness. God has bound Himself to us by His promise of grace. Our hope as Christians is unchangeably fixed. As a servant of God, we come before Him upon the basis of His mercy. It is through the blood of Jesus Christ which was shed for our sins that we can pray, *"Deal with Your servant according to Your mercy"* (verse 124).

"It is time for You to act, O Lord." In this 126th verse, the psalmist has a boldness in his language that seems to summon God to the rescue of His own world. *"...they have regarded Your law as void."* This is not done by the indulgence of sin in action, but in the heart. There are those who are in outright opposition to God's Word and, through their unbelief, break God's laws. However, this area can become a subtle stumbling area for the Christian. When we try to rationalize or minimize the law of God regarding our conduct or actions, we are in danger of breaking God's law. It is a great temptation to apply the law of God to others and exempt ourselves. This weakens both the meaning and authority of what God is saying to us. When we break down in one point, it is easy to compromise and break down in another. When we rationalize our conduct based on the standards set for us by society at large, our conformance can put us beyond the standards of God's laws. Today, there seems to be a blurring of standards, and the indictment is that we neither love good nor hate evil as we should. We must remember that God says, *"I hate every false way"* (verse 128) and that God's promise of judgment is just as sure as His promise of mercy.

I. Psalm 119:129-144

"The entrance of Your words gives light; It gives understanding to the simple." (verse 130). God's Word provides illumination for understanding. His instructions are truly wonderful. They are wonderful in their majesty and purity. God's Word gives us insight into the creation of the world and His eternal purpose for mankind. It provides us with life-giving rules to live by and a promise of life hereafter.

The words *"direct my steps,"* in verse 133, combine two ideas: "regulation" and "establishment". We need a rule of life, and we need to habitually become established with loyalty to that rule. Our spiritual condition most certainly affects our practical lives. *"The steps of a good man are ordered by the Lord"* (Psalm 37:23). Each day our life will exemplify the marks of a Christian in joyful service.

J. Psalm 119:145-160

The royal law is *"You shall love the Lord your God with all your heart, with all your soul, and with all your mind"* (Matthew 22:37). God does not want us to be hesitating or half-hearted. The psalmist prayed "Save me" from sin, temptation and all the hindrances that would keep one from keeping the instructions of the Lord. The prayer is short but from the heart. The psalmist also prayed, *"Plead my cause and redeem me. . ."* (verse 154). If there is an accuser to resist, we have an Advocate to plead our cause of acceptance in the court of heaven. Jesus, our redeemer is pleading our cause for our deliverance. *". . .Revive me according to Your word"* (verse 154). "Revive" means to renew; to bring forth a new spiritual aliveness: more love, more grace, more courage and more strength. It is a desire which cannot be expressed too often. God alone can give us this quickening. *"According to Your Word."* There are two ways of knowing the Lord and they are inseparable: **First**, by the letter of His Word; **second**, by the Spirit's application of the letter of the Word. The light of God's Word and the light of the Holy Spirit are the two lights to guide us.

"...they do not keep Your word" (verse 158). *"Salvation is far from the wicked"* (verse 155) only because they have chosen it to be so. In their pride they have no desire to know God's ways. They say to God, *"Depart from us."* God has made every provision for salvation, but each person must choose to accept or reject that provision. God's mercies are tender and full of compassion. He is rich in mercy to all that call upon Him.

K. Psalm 119:161-176

In the last section of this very beautiful, instructive, and meaningful psalm, the psalmist writes, *"My heart stands in awe of Your Word."* Awe of the Word results in a serious consideration and carefulness about doing anything that would violate or be in contradiction to God's Word. There has been effort to change God's Word to fit what society wants it to say, but God's Word is changeless. It is a set of life-giving rules which apply to all generations. Because society has sought to change the impact of its teaching does not change truth or make the Word less relevant. Many social issues today are the ruin of our society and breed crime and death. God's Word brings justice and life! This is all the more reason why Christians should love it, guard it, teach it and live according to its precepts. Would to God that we all had a compelling love for it which would result in a hunger to study it and that it would become a compelling factor for change in our lives and reverse the awful trend that we see about us today. Biblical illiteracy is the foremost reason for a world being in turmoil. If we are going to live by God's Word, we must know it. As we study, we should be moved to a reverential awe of the Word of God. May this study in Psalms be a challenge for change.

Daily Bible Study Questions for Group Discussion

Note: Read notes and Scripture references before answering the questions. Some questions are for those more advanced in Bible Study. Try to answer all questions but don't be discouraged if some seem a little hard. Unless otherwise instructed, use Bible only in answering questions.

FIRST DAY: Read notes on Lesson 22.

1. After reading the notes, choose one of the following subjects for giving a lesson from this psalm.
    1. Love of God's Word.
    2. Prayer.
    3. Lesson to youth.
    4. Christian living in today's world.

2. List some points for emphasis that might benefit each of us by applying them to our own lives.

3. From either the text, notes or lecture, what was most meaningful to you in the study of **Psalm 119**?

SECOND DAY: Read Psalm 120-123.

4. In **Psalm 120**, what are some of the sources of distress experienced by the psalmist that would be reason for his crying unto the Lord?

5. There are three different words used in **Psalm 121** to express what God is to the psalmist and is also to us. What are the three words?

6. **Psalm 122**. Where were the children of Israel going and for what purpose?

7. When the Israelites were subjected to scorn and contempt, what kept them from despair? **(Psalm 123)**

THIRD DAY: Read Psalm 124-128.

8. Give the phrases describing Israel's trouble in **Psalm 124**.

9. In **Psalm 125**, Mount Zion and the mountains round about Jerusalem speak to God's people of what two things?

10. **Note:** At the time of this writing, the children of Israel had been in captivity in Babylon for seventy years. They were now pilgrims returning to their land of Zion.

   a) What expressions are given in **Psalm 126** that show their ecstatic feelings?

   b) **Verses 5 and 6** have special meaning as to sowing and reaping. Do you have any special thoughts on this?

FOURTH DAY: Read Psalms 127, 128, and 129.

    11. What phrases in **Psalms 127 and 128** describe a happy situation in domestic life?

    12. What is the secret of God's blessing as expressed in **Psalm 128**?

    13. Considering **Psalms 129 verses 1-4**, what two abiding truths are set forth concerning Christians into today's world?

FIFTH DAY: Read Psalm 130, 131, 132; also Romans 3:19-23, 4:7.

    14. Consider **Psalm 130:3** in the setting of a civic court of justice. The individual being tried is found guilty; his sentence severe. An individual standing before God, a righteous judge, is counted as guilty according to God's law. What makes the difference in the two court scenes?

    15. What is the sure foundation upon which the psalmist's hope rests?

    16. What four things does the psalmist say about himself in **Psalm 131**?

17. What was the reason for the zeal and eagerness the psalmist expressed about David in **Psalm 132:1-5**?

SIXTH DAY: Read Psalms 133, 134 and 135.

18. What two similes, in **Psalm 133**, does the psalmist use to bring out the abundant blessing that comes from brethren dwelling *"together in unity."*

19. a) In **Psalms 134 and 135**, who are called upon to praise the Lord?

    b) What reasons are given for praising the Lord? **(verses 3-5)**

20. What verses, in **Psalm 135**, give the ways in which God's greatness is manifested?

21. What is said about idols, their makers, and those who trust in them?

Notes

Explorer's Bible Study

Psalms 120-135

Introduction

Psalms 120-134 are referred to as the "Song of Ascents." These were sung during the periodical journey or pilgrimage to Jerusalem at yearly festivals. This group of psalms is a blending of the joy and sorrow, of the triumph and aspirations which were characteristic of Israel. Some believe the songs were prepared to be sung by the exiles returning from Babylon to Jerusalem. They could well have been suited for both. Originally these psalms existed as a separate hymn book. Bible students love these pilgrim songs.

I. Psalm 120

The psalmist cried to the Lord and his cry was heard. The source of his distress was the lying lips and a deceitful and false tongue. It is not exaggerating to say that a good portion of miseries in life come from a reckless and malignant use of the tongue. Unlike scripture, we judge the sins of the tongue all too lightly. In a previous lesson, we used the text in James chapter three. There are consequences to the use of the tongue. James says, *"Who is wise and understanding among you? Let him show by good conduct that his works are done in the meekness of wisdom. But if you have bitter envy and self-seeking in your hearts, do not boast and lie against the truth"* (James 3:13-14).

II. Psalm 121-122

The Lord is helper, keeper and preserver. This beautiful psalm is the trustful expression of a rejoicing heart under the watchful eye of Him who is both the Maker of heaven and earth and the Keeper of Israel. God is also the One who helps and keeps the individual. The following psalm (122) indicates that it is most probable that this psalm (121) was sung as the evening song by the pilgrims before retiring the last evening on their journey to Jerusalem. The mountains of Jerusalem were within sight at last. They would soon be at the very gates of Zion. The sight filled them with a sense of peace and security. A voice began, *"I will lift up my eyes to the hills; from whence comes my help?"* Another voice answered, *"He will not allow your foot to be moved; He who keeps you will not slumber."* Then the whole company of pilgrims took up the response. *"Behold, He who keeps Israel shall neither slumber nor sleep. The Lord is your keeper."* The following day they sang, *"Our feet have been standing within your gates, O Jerusalem!"* The pilgrims had reached their journey's end; they were in their beloved city, Jerusalem.

Verse one of Psalm 122 is an example of what our approach should be to public worship of God: a spirit of gladness coupled with an appreciation for the privilege of worship. When the pilgrims reached their goal and their feet stood at the gate, the psalmist exclaimed, *"Jerusalem is builded as a city that is compact together."* The city had risen again out of its ruined condition. The psalmist remembered when Jerusalem had been the great religious and political center of the nation: the dwelling place of the Lord and the seat of government for the kings of the house of David. Jerusalem had known a double glory.

The last four verses of this psalm portray the heart of the psalmist in unselfish patriotism — not for his sake only, but for the sake of his brethren, his people. For the sake of His God, His temple, and His service, he desired peace for Jerusalem and called upon others to pray for the peace of Jerusalem.

III. Psalm 123

This psalm is a psalm of sighing. The sighing is a result of being exposed to scorn and contempt. This psalm was written either while the psalmist was in exile near the end of the captivity, or after returning to his native land only to endure further scorn and contempt by the Samaritans and others. Compare Nehemiah 2:19, *"They laughed at us and despised us"* with verse 4 of this psalm, *". . .the scorn of those who are at ease, with the contempt of the proud."* The eyes of the psalmist were directed upward to the hand of God, looking only to Him and no other for help. He was looking in faith and patience for God's deliverance.

IV. Psalm 124

In Psalms 123-125, we have three successive pictures, or rather three pieces which comprise one picture. They are not only linked together as representing successive scenes in one history, but they are also pervaded by one great master thought which lends its unity to the whole group. In each, there is the same full recognition of God's grace and power working both for the deliverance and security of His people. Psalm 124 recorded the feelings of the exiles when the proclamation of Cyrus permitted God's people to return to their native land.

The returned captives were few and poor. They returned to a land destroyed by fire and sword and overrun by wild beasts. The city had been reduced to a heap of ruins. The secret of their strength lay in their trust in God.

He had delivered them from Babylon. He would now sustain and guard them.

The psalm consists of two parts:

1. Verses 1-5: An acknowledgment of God as the deliverer of Israel.

2. Verses 6-8: A determination to trust in Him exclusively for future favors.

The whole psalm is alive with joy: the joy of an escape and of a triumph. The psalmist is joyful in what God had done for His people. The first division of the psalm opens with a confession that if the Lord had not been on their side, they would have been swallowed up and overwhelmed. The second division opens with a thanksgiving to the Lord, who had not given them as a prey to the teeth of their enemy. The Psalm closes with an affirmation. As we encounter times of struggle in our lives, may we remember

and be able to affirm as the psalmist did, *"Our help is in the name of the Lord, who made heaven and earth."*

V. Psalm 125

Those who trust in the Lord will stand firm as Zion itself. They are like a mountain which cannot be shaken. They "abide forever" because of their foundation. They are steadfast in the Lord, the God of the covenant and of its promises. *"As the mountains surround Jerusalem, so the Lord surrounds His people from this time forth and forever."* In verse 3 the "secpter" is an emblem of authority or power and the "land allotted" represents all that makes up the state of the righteous. This passage is stating that God will not permit the wicked to hold power over the righteous. This is a manifestation of God's care over His people. God would not leave them forever under the rod of the wicked. His people had suffered under the proud rule of Babylon and in mercy God delivered them. The Lord is ever mindful of our frailty. He remembers that we are but dust and prone to sin. When oppression and trials from the wicked bring us low and make us cry to the Lord, it is then that we honor His grace and power, His truth and His love. We pledge our love and faithfulness to the promise to love Him with all our heart, soul and mind. The psalmist prayed for all good to be given to the good, but for those who turn aside from righteous ways, he prayed for the Lord to give them their portion according to their works.

VI. Psalm 126

The first group of exiles had returned to Israel. The permission to return had been unexpected. When it came, the people could hardly believe it. To those who found themselves actually restored to the land of Zion, it seemed like a dream. It was a joy beyond expressing. God had performed a miracle for them and even the heathen recognized the hand of Israel's God in this event. It is with these thoughts that this beautiful psalm opens.

Just a small remnant had formed the first caravan. Because of this, the psalmist prayed *"Bring back our captivity, O Lord, as the streams in the South."* The returned exiles experienced much discouragement and opposition. It was a time of sowing in tears.

Still, faith could expect a joyful harvest. The children of Israel recognized their deliverance as the work of God and gave Him the glory, saying, *"The Lord has done great things for us, and we are glad."* Their joy was expressed in laughter and singing. Even the heathen around them ceased their scoffing and said, "The Lord hath done great things for them." The hope of being restored to their homeland, after seventy years, had seemed a remote probability. There is no record of any nation, other than Israel, returning from a captivity to their homeland to rebuild their cities and homes.

The Christian is called by God's message, redeemed by the blood of the Son of God and renewed by the power of the Holy Spirit. We too can say as the psalmist, *"The Lord has done great things for us, and we are glad."*

The exiles that returned to their homeland were but few compared to others of their brethren who were still to come. Their prayer was *"Turn again our captivity O Lord as the streams in the south."* They prayed that God would continue to bring back their captive brethren who were still in Babylon.

"He who continually goes forth weeping, bearing seed for sowing, shall doubtless come again with rejoicing, bringing his sheaves with him" (verse 6). The seed that is sown and watered with tears of the sower brings a sure and glorious harvest. Tears are often God's path to a blessed harvest. We are called upon as God's servants to be faithful in sowing the precious seed of the Word. The results are in God's hands. Missionaries often spend years of sowing the Word seeing few results. There are present disappointments, but there will be a harvest. Isaiah 55:11 says, *"So shall My word be that goes forth from My mouth; It shall not return to Me void, but it shall accomplish what I please, and it shall prosper in the thing for which I sent it."* The harvest belongs to God. God's call to us is faithfulness to Him in service. The joy of life's ripe harvest is the good of our hopes. Jesus said, *"Most assuredly, I say to you, unless a grain of wheat falls into the ground and dies, it remains alone; but if it dies, it produces much grain"* (John 12:24). *"Looking unto Jesus, the author and finisher of our faith, who for the joy that was set before Him endured the cross,* *despising the shame, and has sat down at the right hand of the throne of God"* (Hebrews 12:2).

VII. Psalm 127

This psalm and the following Psalm 128 are companion pictures of social and domestic life. They depict the happiness of a household which, trained in the fear of God, is blessed by His providence. *"Unless the Lord builds the house, they labor in vain who build it"* (Psalm 127:1). It is foolish to undertake projects that leave no time for rest and comfort; no time for family or friends. Duties are ours, events are God's and duties should be free from anxiety because we trust in the Lord. He will give us all that we have need of. Make sure that the building of projects does not rob you of time with God and with your family. You may accomplish your project but suffer losses in your spiritual life as well as your domestic life. God is important, husband and wife are important and your children are important. We need to pray that God will give us a balance in priorities. Anxiety can cause friction, irritability and creates problems in families. Striving for things resulting in a build-up of debt are the building blocks of anxiety and potential domestic problems. Remember, *"Unless the Lord builds the house, they labor in vain who build it."* The psalmist did not suggest that the builder stop his labor nor suggest that the watchmen should neglect their duty. The warning is against putting our trust in our work alone. Unless what we do is to God's glory, even for our domestic situations, all human effort will be in vain. As Christians, it is good to keep in mind that the Lord is concerned about everything which touches our lives.

I believe verse two of Psalm 127 is saying that no one should work beyond his physical and intellectual ability, nor beyond the hours which nature allots. A feverish straining, as if toil itself could command success, brings undue anxiety. A job is always done better if we are physically and spiritually prepared for each day.

"Behold, children are a heritage from the Lord." The psalmist spoke of what children are to godly parents. Children are His heritage and are precious in His sight. What a privilege and responsibility it is to raise our children for the Lord.

This psalm reminds us that we depend on God for the blessings we most covet and prize: the happiness of home and the success of our labors. It makes us mindful that we build in vain unless God builds with us and we watch in vain unless God watches with us. It rebukes feverish anxiety which exhausts our energies and makes life hard and bitter to us.

VIII. Psalm 128

This psalm is a picture of the family happiness of one who fears God and leads a holy life. Israel and Jerusalem are considered in their relation to domestic life and as contributing to its happiness. How true it is that through destroying the family, you destroy a nation. The truly happy man and happy family is one who fears the Lord, not just in profession, but one who walks in His ways doing His commandments. We are promised blessing upon hard and honest work. Although we are in God's hands, we are to be supported by our own hands. God will give us daily bread, but it must be made our own by labor. The promise is that labor will be fruitful. Even if it were possible for us to have what we desire without work or effort, our enjoyment of those things would be severly limited. We only appreciate that which is a result of our own self-denial and labor. In both temporal and spiritual things, we should not so depend upon the grace of God as to neglect the part we have ourselves to act upon. God crowns every honest and faithful effort with success. *"When you eat the labor of your hands, you shall be happy, and it shall be well with you."*

"Your wife shall be like a fruitful vine in the very heart of your house, your children like olive plants all around your table." The general structure of an Oriental house is a court with a fountain and garden around the inner walls of which run an arched colonnade. Under the arches are doors which open into the living rooms. Those arches and walls often have climbing plants, with blooming flowers. The psalmist compared the wife to a vine which beautifies the inner sides of the court. The vine represents not only fruitfulness, but also grace and cheerfulness. The children are compared to "olive plants" because the olive was a recognized Hebrew symbol of vigor, health and joy.

God specifically designed the male and the female with differing characteristics which correspond to the different responsibilities of the husband and the wife. Both are vital to the family structure. Both bring unique qualities that are needed in the family unit. The terms superior or inferior are not properly applicable. It should also be recognized that each child contributes something to this family unit. Whenever you see the home of a married couple that defies every domestic storm, and they are sure to come, you can be sure that the marriage rests upon a sure foundation, and that foundation is the fear of the Lord. The family that studies God's Word, prays and lives by His precepts, will be blessed.

"Yes, may you see your children's children. Peace be upon Israel!" This is a promise of long life. The family was designed in the beginning by the direct act of God and with His special blessing. The sacred union of husband and wife is the source of all domestic happiness. Jesus taught the sacredness and permanence of the marriage covenant, and added, *"What therefore, God has joined together, let not man put asunder."* To degrade marriage, degrades man and dishonors God. The home is the target of Satan's destructive work and for obvious reasons, it is a threat to his evil designs. God wants us to live in an atmosphere of love and forgiveness building a home on a sure foundation. Building is not done in a day but by daily adorning the structure with great care to make a happy and beautiful home for the glory of God.

IX. Psalm 129

The nation Israel, delivered from captivity in Babylon, could look back through their history and see the great law of suffering and yet see God's tokens of mercy. Their past is a record of conflict but also a record of victory (verse 2). The great principle on which Israel's final victory rests is the righteousness of God (verse 4). God had delivered them from bondage in Babylon. Full of thankfulness for deliverance, the psalmist hoped for the overthrow of their oppressors to be complete and final.

There are two divisions in the psalm:

1. The record of the past (verses 1-4).

2. The prayer which is also a hope for the future (verses 5-8).

X. Psalm 130

This psalm is a cry to God for the forgiveness of sin. The psalmist had waited upon God and trusted in His word. He encouraged all Israel to hope, to wait and to look for God's mercy and redemption.

On one occasion Luther was asked which were the best psalms, he replied: "The Pauline Psalms, and being pressed to say which they were, he answered: "The thirty-second, the fifty-first, the one hundred and thirtieth, and the one hundred and forty-third; for they teach us that the forgiveness of sins is vouchsafed to them that believe, without the law and without works; therefore are they Pauline Psalms; and when David sings,

'With Thee is forgiveness, that Thou mayest be feared,' so Paul likewise saith, 'God hath concluded all under sin, that He may have mercy on all.' Therefore none can boast of his own righteousness; but the words, 'That Thou mayest be feared,' thrust away all self- merit and teach us to confess that it is all forgiveness and no merit" (Luther).

This psalm reveals the two great roots of Christian theology, that of sin and forgiveness. *"If You, Lord, should mark iniquities, O Lord, who could stand?"* and *"But there is forgiveness with You, that You may be feared."* We need to be assured of God's unlimited compassion because it is against him that we have sinned. We need assurance that He does not watch for our iniquities that He might condemn us, but that He may redeem us. For this truth this psalm is valuable and precious.

XI. Psalm 131

The previous psalm is a song of forgiveness. This psalm is a song of humility. The previous celebrates the blessedness of the man whose transgressions are pardoned. This one celebrates the blessedness of those who are of a meek and lowly spirit. Forgiveness should humble us. When one speaks of being forgiven, it implies a sin was committed and a request and acceptance of forgiveness in humility. It is in good order that the psalm of humility follows the psalm which sings of God's loving-kindness and tender mercies.

XII. Psalm 132

This psalm is a prayer that God's promises made to David would be fulfilled, that God would dwell forever in the habitation which He chose for Himself in Zion, and that the children of David would sit upon His throne forever. The psalm opens with a description of David's efforts to bring the ark to its resting place in Jerusalem. It ends by relating the promises made to David and to his seed.

The psalm has two divisions:

1. Verses 1-10: The toil that went before the completion of the temple and prayer for God's blessing on it at its completion.

2. Verses 11-18: A prayer that David's efforts may be rewarded by the fulfillment of the promise to him and to his house. God's answer is guaranteed by His oath.

The afflictions referred to in this psalm were the anxiety and distress David felt in striving to reunite the Ark and tabernacle, and then to build a more permanent sanctuary. This zeal for the house of God is one of the most characteristic features in the history of David. He was rewarded for this, not only with a promise that his son should build the temple but that God would build a house for him by granting a perpetual succession in his family upon the throne of Judah.

The only reasonable explanation of verse 6 is that which makes Ephratah the ancient name for Bethlehem (Genesis 48:7). It is possible that David spent his youth there and it was where he had first heard of the Ark of the Covenant. The general scope of the passage in verses 1 to 5 seems to be, "Remember Thy servant David; remember his efforts to build your house for your name;" he did not rest till he brought the ark to Zion. He heard where the Ark was and he went to get it (v.6). *"For Your servant David's sake, do not turn away the face of Your Anointed. The Lord has sworn in truth to David; He will not turn from it: I will set upon your throne the fruit of your body"* (vs.10-11).

Verses 7 to 9 brings a transition. The Ark had been brought to its destination and all was ready for worship. The public prayer was now that God Himself would arise and come into this place of His abiding. His abiding place was the seat of His visible presence (the Shekinah) above the mercy-seat upon the lid of the Ark of the covenant and underneath the cherubim. The words of this prayer, in verses 8 and 9, are those used by Solomon at the dedication of the first temple where the Ark was first consecrated. The prayer was an invocation for God's presence to abide there. *"Now therefore, Arise, O Lord God, to Your resting place, You and the ark of Your strength. Let Your priests, O Lord God, be clothed with salvation, and let Your saints rejoice in goodness"* (II Chronicles 6:41). It is important today for our prayers to be that those who minister in God's house be clothed with salvation and righteousness. "Do not lose the force of this petition by thinking that 'righteousness' is a hazy theological virtue, having little to do with every-day life and little resemblance to secular morality. To be gentle and just, loving and truthful, self-forgetting and self-ruling, honest and true, kind and helpful, to live in the exercise of the virtues, which the con-sciences and tongues of all men call lovely and of good report, and to add to them all the consecration of reference of Him in whom these parted graces dwell united and complete - this is to be righteous, as the psalmist conceived it. Remember that growing purity in life and deed is the main proof that Christ's righteousness is indeed ours. If we are to do God's work in the world, we must be good, true, righteous men" (Alexander Maclaren D. D.). There can be no assault on evil unless we are armed with holy lives.

The kingdom of Judah might have continued had its kings been faithful to the Lord. When the royal house of David fell, it did so because of its continual sinning against God. The people and rulers of Judah provoked the Lord for many years, but He was longsuffering. Long after the northern kingdom Israel had gone into captivity, Judah still remained. God continually showed His miracles of mercy to her. His patience exceeded all limits, for the Lord's regard for David was great. The princes of David's house seemed determined to ruin themselves. Man's breach of promise caused the covenant to fail. Yet in spirit and essence, the Lord has been true to His covenant for Jesus reigns and holds the throne forever. He is the Anointed One of God. In Him is the fulfillment of all the shadows and types of the Old Testament.

XIII. Psalm 133

This psalm is expressive of the truth and beauty which all desire. *"Behold, how good and how pleas-ant it is for brethren to dwell together in unity!"* Separation, isolation and discord are all displeasing to God. To appreciate this rich gift of God, we think of it in terms of a peaceful family. The church may also be considered as a family. It should be in the family unit where we learn to dwell together in unity. We must learn the art of true love, understanding and discipline. We must each learn to do our part to contribute to an atmosphere of making things better that there may be peace and harmony in the home as well as the church family.

The illustration given in verses 2 and 3 of the pleasantness of unity is expressed in the likeness of precious ointment being poured upon the head and running down to the skirts of Aaron's garment. This consecration of our whole selves is likened to having our whole person saturated with the pervading fra-grance of a precious ointment. The second illustration expressive of the blessing of the pleasantness of unity in family and church is taken from the dew. It falls alike on both Mt. Herman and upon the mountain of Zion which is a lower mountain than Herman. The oil goes from the head to the beard; the dew from the higher mountain to the lower. As the oil sanctified the whole body, so by the dew the whole land was united and blessed. Love is the uniting and sanctifying force of life. Christians being blessed by God are a blessing to others. The world observes the strife and disunity within both the Christian family and the Church. This gives occasion for Satan to blaspheme the Christ we represent. The world is always ready to use any means, expecially a stumbling or failure of any professed believer to discredit all. Believers in strife are a weakened body, and that is exactly what Satan wants. If there was ever a time in the history of Christianity that we need to be strong, it is today. To fragment lessens our witness for Christ in a world that is decaying and dying. We need to pray that God will give us a renewed vision of what the objectives of the Church should be and a burden to accomplish these objectives. We can be so busy soothing and settling problems and strife within the body of believers that there are missed opportunities for reaching out to those who need Christ. False religions and cults are on the rise only because the Church has moved aside and given them reason and space to be born and grow. May we not give time to envy and strife which causes us to lose the battle. May we, instead, be challenged as believers to possess what God has given us.

XIV. Psalm 134

The series of pilgrim songs closes with this psalm—a summons to bless the Lord. First, there is a greeting and then a reply. The greeting is addressed to the priests and Levites who had the night watch of the temple. This psalm was placed at the end of the collection of pilgrim songs to take the place of a final blessing. This psalm teaches us to pray for those who are ministering before the Lord, and it invites all ministers to give a benediction on their loving and prayerful people.

XV. Psalm 135

This psalm was intended for the temple service. Like Psalm 134, it is an exhortation to the priests and Levites who wait in the sanctuary to praise God for His goodness in choosing Israel to be His people;

for His greatness and almighty power shown in His dominion over the world of nature and in the overthrow of all the enemies of His people. The Lord's abiding majesty was contrasted with the nothingness of the idols of the heathen. This psalm is almost entirely composed of passages taken from other sources in the psalms.

This psalm has six divisions:

1. Verses 1-4: The people are exhorted to praise God.

2. Verses 5-7: To praise God as the God of nature and Creator.

3. Verses 8-12: Praise God as the deliverer of Israel from the land of Egypt and in Canaan.

4. Verses 13-14: God as their hope for the present and for the future.

5. Verses 15-18: God, more glorious by contrast with the emptiness of idols.

6. Verses 19-21: The psalm concludes as it began with an exhortation to praise God.

Daily Bible Study Questions for Group Discussion

Note: Read notes and Scripture references before answering the questions. Some questions are for those more advanced in Bible Study. Try to answer all questions but don't be discouraged if some seem a little hard. Unless otherwise instructed, use Bible only in answering questions.

FIRST DAY: Read notes on Lesson 23.

1. List several subjects found in **Psalms 120-135** that are helpful to Christian living.

2. a) What psalm reveals the two great roots of Christian theology?

   b) What are those roots?

3. What psalm or verse from this lesson was most meaningful to you?

SECOND DAY: Read Psalm 136-137.

4. There are two parts to **Psalm 136**. Give verses for each part:
   a) Referring to the God of Creation, verses _____.

   b) Referring to the God of deliverance and redemption,
      verses_____ .

5. **Psalm 137** is a reminiscence of the sad scenes of one who had returned from captivity in Babylon. Besides having to leave their homeland, what situation added to their sorrow?

6. How strongly did they feel about remembering their homeland, Jerusalem?

THIRD DAY: Read Psalm 138-139.

7. Besides prayer, praise and worship to God, what else is mentioned in **Psalm 138** that is a factor in changing our life to be what God wants us to be?

8. What verse in **Psalm 138** is a promise and an encouragment to us?

9. a) When we read **Psalm 139**, what do we learn about God?

    b) After considering God as the all knowing One, what meaning should the prayer in **verses 23 and 24 of Psalm 139** have for us?

FOURTH DAY: Read Psalm 140 to 143.

10. a) The psalmist gives a description of his enemies in **Psalm 140**. In your text work sheet underline with colored pen or pencil (1) their character (2) their method (3) their purpose.

    b) What does the psalmist do about his enemies?

11. In **Psalm 141:5**, what correction was the psalmist willing to receive if only he might be kept from sin?

12. a) From the petition of the psalmist in **Psalm 143:7-11**, make a list of what he needed God to do for him. (First two words of each verse)

    b) Could all such petitions be included in one's daily prayer?

FIFTH DAY: Read Psalms 144 to 147.

13. In **verse 3 of Psalm 144** David prayed, *"Lord, what is man, that You take knowledge of him? Or the son of man, that You are mindful of him?"* There are numerous verses in the New Testament which assure us of the high value God placed on us. List a few of these verses. (Example: John 3:16).

14. **Read Psalm 145** carefully and prayerfully. Think about why God should be praised and what should praise Him. Give a favorite verse from this psalm.

15. **Read Psalm 146:7-9**. How many of these statements find fulfillment in the miracles and ministry of Christ in the Gospels?

16. Which verse in **Psalm 147** tells us what pleases God?

SIXTH DAY: Read Psalm 148-150.

17. The call to praise is inclusive of both heaven and earth. What reason is given in the last verses of **Psalm 148** as to why all should praise the Lord?

18. What two methods of music were used by God's people in praising the Lord?

Psalm 140

1 Deliver me, O LORD, from evil men; Preserve me from violent men,

2 Who plan evil things in their hearts; They continually gather together for war.

3 They sharpen their tongues like a serpent; The poison of asps is under their lips. Selah

4 Keep me, O LORD, from the hands of the wicked; Preserve me from violent men, Who have purposed to make my steps stumble.

5 The proud have hidden a snare for me, and cords; They have spread a net by the wayside; They have set traps for me. Selah

6 I said to the LORD: "You are my God; Hear the voice of my supplications, O LORD.

7 O GOD the Lord, the strength of my salvation, You have covered my head in the day of battle.

8 Do not grant, O LORD, the desires of the wicked; Do not further his wicked scheme, Lest they be exalted. Selah

9 "As for the head of those who surround me, Let the evil of their lips cover them;

10 Let burning coals fall upon them; Let them be cast into the fire, Into deep pits, that they rise not up again.

11 Let not a slanderer be established in the earth; Let evil hunt the violent man to overthrow him."

12 I know that the LORD will maintain The cause of the afflicted, And justice for the poor.

13 Surely the righteous shall give thanks to Your name; The upright shall dwell in Your presence.

Notes

Psalms 136-150

I. Psalm 136

This psalm is somewhat a variation and repetition of the preceding psalm. The first line of each verse pursues the theme of the psalm. The second line, *"For His mercy endures forever"* is a refrain or response. The first line would be sung by some of the Levites and the second by the choir or by the whole congregation together with the Levites.

This psalm has two divisions:

1. Verses 1-9: Praise to God for His works of creation.

   a. Praise for what He is (verses 1-3).

   b. Praise for what He is able to do (verse 4).

   c. Praise for what He has done in creation (verses 5-9).

2. Verses 10-26: Praise to God for His works of redemption.

   a. Praise for what He did in redeeming Israel from bondage (verses 10-15).

   b. Praise for what He did in His providence toward them (verses 16-22).

   c. Praise for His grace in times of calamity (verses 23-24).

   d. Praise for His grace to the world at large (verse 25).

   e. Praise that God is the God of heaven (verse 26) (Source - A. Bonar.)

II. Psalm 137

After the psalms of praise and thanksgiving, there is a song relating to the time when Zion lay in ruins. The songs of the Levite choir were hushed. This psalmist is one who had recently returned from the captivity. Upon seeing the devastation of his nation's land, he was overwhelmed with the memories of the capture and being taken to Babylon. He first sang of the sad scene of the exile. Then he sang of the desire of the exiles that they might join in the worhip which had been the privilege of their fathers in the city of Jerusalem.

The psalm is divided into three parts:

1. Verses 1-3: The sorrow of the exiles in their remembrance of Zion. It would be doing violence to their most sacred feelings to comply with the demands of their proud oppressors to sing to them the songs of Zion.

2. Verses 4-6: The determination of the exiles never to profane the Lord's songs by singing them in a foreign land and never to forget their beloved city.

3. Verses 7-9: The call for destruction upon the Edomites for their cruel conduct at the time Jerusalem was destroyed, and also upon the Babylonians for their oppressive acts; their cruelties toward the Jews during captivity. It is little wonder that the psalmist would vent his wrath when he looked upon the ruins and wasted fields and remembered the devastation of the invader. The psalmist concluded with a fierce outburst of resentment. He called for revenge upon those who took part in the day of Jerusalem's fall and upon those (the Edomites) who rejoiced in Jerusalem's overthrow when they should have come to her aid. He called for revenge upon the proud oppressors who had held Jerusalem captive and made their hearts bitter. The wrongs to Jerusalem had been terrible — let the revenge be terrible.

The Jews were punished for their apostasy by being carried as captives to Babylon; their city and temple were destroyed by fire. Their captivity lasted for seventy years and the cruelties experienced during captivity were great. The last two verses of the psalm, although shocking to Christian sensibilities, are to be read with an understanding of the time in which the psalmist lived. By the customs of ancient warfare, these vindictive requests were an expression of the desire for victory over an enemy. According to the barbarous standards of those days, the slaughter of infants belonged to the practice of war when a fortress had been bombarded by the enemy. The imprecations in the psalms should not be judged by the more merciful feelings which Christianity has introduced into the code of war; neither should they be taken for the mere cry of personal or rational revenge. The Jews had identified their capital and kingdom with the kingdom of God upon earth. An assault upon these was a double crime — a crime against the people and a crime of sacrilege and rebellion against God. Their patriotism was intensified by their religious faith. This is expressed in the preceding verses of the psalm. The Jews had been taken to a land of great beauty, and though they were captives, the way to wealth and advancement was open to them if they would adopt the country and its customs. Instead, they chose to cling to the memory of their beloved Zion. Though Jerusalem had been burned and its walls destroyed to their foundations, it was still to them the most precious spot on earth. Nothing caused them to forget the sorrows of the Lord's house. This should be meaningful for us today. We should value the kingdom of God above all our joys, and whatever happens in the name of Christ and Christianity should be a personal concern to all Christians. Our privileges and freedom in Christ could be threatened and lost should we treat them carelessly. Israel went into captivity because they did not follow the Lord and His Word. They had not totally left the worship of God, but they had added idolatry. They tried to have it both ways.

III. Psalm 138

Psalms 138 to 145 were composed in the first person and are the Israelite's manual for private prayer and praise.

This psalm has three divisions:

1. Verses 1-3: Praise to God for His goodness, faithfulness and great promises. Praise for prayers answered.

2. Verses 4-6: The hope and the prophecy that the kings of the earth shall acknowledge the greatness of God. God measures greatness and lowliness by standards which are different than human standards.

3. Verses 7-8: God's character when one who trusts in Him is in trouble or danger.

Praise was the main focus of David's worship; the name or character of God the great object of his song.

"For You have magnified Your word above all Your name" (verse 2). Greater than God's work is the Word by which a lost world is redeemed. It is the "Word" that He has magnified above all His name, showing the exceeding greatness of His power, His wisdom and the glories of His holiness and love.

"The Lord will perfect that which concerns me: Your mercy, O Lord, endures forever; do not forsake the works of Your hands" (verse 8). *"Being confident of this very thing, that He who has begun a good work in you will complete it until the day of Jesus Christ"* (Phillipians 1:6). The stability of grace and perseverance is founded on God's unchangeableness. It is a dishonor to God to question His promises. He wants us as His children to put all our trust in His mercy and His goodness. He will help us to live a life that is always growing toward that which is preparing us for God's best.

IV. Psalm 139

No other place in all of Scripture emphasizes the attributes of God to the extent they are emphasized here. His omniscience (knowledge or all knowing); His omnipresence (all present or everywhere present); His omnipotence (all powerful or almighty) are all set forth in this psalm. There is the overwhelming sense of the fact that man is compassed about by God, pervaded by His Spirit. We are the workmanship of God. We stand in the presence and under the eye of One who is our Judge. The power of our conscience and the sense of sin and responsibility is felt and acknowledged. Prayer is offered to One who is not only the

Judge, but a Friend, to One who is feared as no one else is feared; to One who is loved as no one else is loved.

There are four divisions in the psalm, each consisting of six verses:

1. Verses 1-6: The omniscience of God as manifested in His knowledge of the deepest thoughts and most secret workings of the human heart.

2. Verses 7-12: The omnipresence of God. There is no corner of the universe so remote that it is not pervaded by God's presence; no darkness so deep that it can hide from His eyes.

3. Verses 13-18: The reason for the profound conviction of these truths. It is no wonder that God should have intimate knowledge of us, for we are His creatures. The mysterious beginnings of life cannot be traced apart from God. The days, all of which are ordered before the first breath is drawn, are all fashioned and ordered by the hand of God.

4. Verses 19-24: The psalmist abruptly changed subjects. He expressed his abhorrence of wicked men—an abhorrence no doubt deepened by the previous meditation about God and His attributes. The psalmist closed with a prayer that in his innermost heart he would be right with God who had searched him and known him and laid His hand upon Him in the way everlasting.

We ought to live each day with the thought that God's eye is upon us. If for no other reason than for the reason that it is reality. When we think of God's eye being upon us, we tend to think in terms of restraint—sometimes requested in the hour of temptation and sometimes acknowledged grudgingly in times of carelessness. But this selfish notion causes us to miss God's best for us. God's eye is upon us not just to restrain us, but to be the greatest and most unfailing comfort. His eye is not the eye of a Judge and Ruler only, but of a Shepherd and Father, the Lover of our souls. We are being watched by an eye of tenderness and sympathy. The depth of this tenderness and sympathy is deeper and truer than even that of our dearest and best friend on earth.

"Do not I hate them, O Lord, who hate You? And do I not loathe those who rise up against You?" (verse 21). God hates sin, and as Christians, we should hate what God hates and love what He loves. God does not hate the person, but hates the person's sins. We are not to hate others because of their evil practices or to love the evil for the sake of those who do evil. The psalmist counted God's enemies as his enemies. Loving and seeking that which is good also involves despising that which is wickedness. There cannot be a genuine pursuit of purity and holiness combined with a tolerance of evil or a desire for it. The attempt to follow the right without breaking with the wrong is what leads to failure on the part of half-hearted Christians. Progress cannot be made in the service and knowledge of God unless we pursue it and have a longing desire to forsake the old life, its influences, associations, practices, indulgences and habits that are against God which keep us from fellowship with Him.

In the last verses, the psalmist appealed to God for the purity of his intentions. He desired to be led in the way of life eternal. The real prayer of faith says, *"Search me, O God, and know my heart: try me, and know my anxieties: and see if there is any wicked way in me, and lead me in the way everlasting"* (verses 23-24). That prayer, sincerely offered, never fails. It asks God to root out all self-will, subside inordinate desire and to bring our will into harmony with His will. Such a prayer stands on the sure and broad foundation of "Thy will be done."

V.   Psalm 140

This psalm was a prayer for protection from enemies who were violent and crafty in the use of their tongues. The psalmist described his adversaries who were preparing themselves for war against him as serpent-like, treacherous and slanderous. It is thought that David wrote this at the time of Absalom's rebellion.

David's hope was in the Lord and he committed all of his circumstance into God's hands. The lips of his enemies had threatened him like a company of greedy hounds. They had purposed to pursue him until they could overtake him. However, David ended his psalm with an expression of his confidence in God.

VI. Psalm 141

This psalm presents some difficulty for interpretation because the specific circumstance under which the Psalm was written is not known. It may have been written by David at the time of his persecution by Saul when he had to flee from Jerusalem. He had been cut off from the sacrificial worship of God. This was probably a psalm written in the evening of a day when David had experienced a great deal of trouble.

"Set a guard, O Lord, over my mouth; keep watch over the door of my lips." Our lips are a door to our words. We too should pray as the psalmist that God's grace would keep that door; that no word would go from our lips that would dishonor God or hurt others.

VII. Psalm 142

This is the last of the eight psalms that refer to David's persecution by Saul. David described his thoughts and feelings when he was in the cave. The expressions used in the psalm are typical of those used by David: cleaving of the heart to God, the deep sense of loneliness, the cry for deliverance, the confidence that deliverance will call faith, sympathy and joy from others.

VIII. Psalm 143

In this psalm, the psalmist petitioned God for an answer to his prayer based on two reasons: God's faithfulness to His promises and His righteousness. His petition was that his character would be vindicated before men. With this petition, came the realization that before the just Judge no person is guiltless. The psalmist cried, *"Do not enter into judgement with Your servant, for in Your sight no one living is righteous."* The afflictions of the psalmist had made him look within and had shown him his own heart in its sinfulness and misery. This deep sense of sin led him to the prayer of verse 2. His deliverance from his enemy and the forgiveness of his sin were connected in his mind. This caused a feeling of emptiness. He remembered the days past in which he had felt God's presence. He meditated upon the redemptive work of God and considered all His mighty and gracious deeds. He considered the work of God's hands. In remembering the past and comparing it to

the present, the psalmist prayed, *"answer me speedily"* (verse 7).

"Cause me to hear Your lovingkindness. . ." (verse 8). Lovingkindness is a favorite expression throughout the psalms. It means to love showing kindness *". . .cause me to know the way in which I should walk."* Think of that which is to be believed, to be renounced, to be examined, or to be distinguished from other things. There are matters to be tentatively dealt with. There are things to be done and left undone. Sometimes we need to move ahead, but sometimes we need to wait. All are included in *"the way in which I should walk."* We deal with opinions, beliefs, conduct, convictions and principles on a daily basis. The secret of knowing "the way" is to commit our lives each day to the Lord and to pray for His wisdom and guidance. We need to walk in the confidence that He is answering our prayers: prayers for deliverance from danger and difficulty, prayers for a teachable spirit and prayers to be quickened in every situation for His name's sake. It is an art to learn to live with such commitment. God has promised to be with us in every situation. Believing God and His Word brings joy in serving Him and brings a positive approach to the Christian life. Remember, we are unable to proceed positively into a day when we have personally failed to meet God before it begins.

IX. Psalm 144

Verses 1-11 consist almost entirely of quotations from other Scripture. Verses 12-15 are in original verse and may have been written after the return from the exile. The objective of the writer seems to have been to revive the hope of his nation by reminding them of their history and how obedience brought its recompense. The psalmist related glorious victories of the past. He complained that the nation was now troubled by strange and cruel enemies so false and treacherous that no covenant could be kept with them. He prayed for deliverance and anticipated the return to former days of peace and plenty.

X. Psalm 145

This psalm is the first of the series of doxology psalms with which the Book of Psalms closes. It is called a praise psalm and consists of three divisions:

1. Verses 1-7: God's greatness and goodness.

2. Verses 8-14: God's grace and kingdom.

3. Verses 15-21: God's readiness to hear and answer the prayers of His people.

Each generation is to praise God's works to the next generation. Each generation treasures the history and songs handed down; then adds its own history and songs of worship and praise. The glorious praises of God can never be exhausted or lessened for He will ever be rich in mercy to all generations. The memory we have of God's goodness is always a source of praise. All God's works shall praise Him and His saints shall bless Him (verse 10). God is recognized as All in All. Wherever we go, His testimony is there. Creation, in all its length and breadth, its depth and height, is the manifestation of His Spirit. His kingdom is a kingdom of grace.

God wants every Christian to be a messenger preaching the Word of life. "*They shall speak of the glory of Your kingdom, and talk of Your power*" (verse 11). Christians are instructors of God's Word both through actions and words. God's people are also a praying people. God, who prepares His people's heart to pray, prepares also His own to hear. "*The Lord preserves all who love Him*" (verse 20). We keep Him in our love, and He keeps us by His love.

XI. Psalm 146

The closing psalms call for universal praise of God. The whole of the visible and rational as well as the invisible and irrational creation is summoned to praise the Lord. Praise him for His blessings upon the earth, for His glories in the heavens, and for His ever watchful and sustaining providence. Praise Him for His wisdom and power, His goodness and especially for His sovereign mercy to us. Praise Him for His love and mercy to His people. For all these blessings and hopes, the psalmist exhorted all people to respond in grateful praise.

XII. Psalm 147

This psalm has special reference to the restoration of Jerusalem after the captivity in Babylon. It was probably used at the celebration of the joyful event recorded in Nehemiah 12:27-43 — the dedication of the wall at Jerusalem.

The four remaining psalms (147-150) are distinguished from the previous psalms by their joyous tone. They each begin and end with "*Hallelujah*" or "*Praise the Lord.*" They were composed to celebrate God's almighty and gracious rule over His people and the world of nature. Mingled with this was a special commemoration of His goodness in bringing His people back from their captivity and rebuilding the walls of Jerusalem. The dedication of the wall was celebrated "*with gladness, both with thanksgivings and singing, with cymbals and stringed instruments and harps*" (Nehemiah 12:27). Some authors suggest that not only Psalm 147 but the rest of the psalms to the end of the book are all anthems originally composed for the same occasion. The walls of Jerusalem had been rebuilt under difficult and discouraging circumstances (Nehemiah 2:17 to 4:23). Its completion was celebrated with great joy and thankfulness, "*for God had made them rejoice with great joy; the women and the children also rejoiced; so that the joy of Jerusalem was heard afar off*" (Nehemiah 12:43).

Psalm 147 — Thankfulness to God for the restoration of Jerusalem which was once again a city with walls and gates. Psalm 148 — Praise to God for the restoration of the national independence. Psalm 149 — Praise to God for their restoration. They who were once defenseless and enslaved had been made capable of joyously and victoriously defending themselves.

XIII. Psalm 148

The psalmist called upon the whole creation, both heaven and earth, to praise the Lord. Things with and things without life, rational and irrational, were all summoned to join in the "Hallelujah" chorus. This psalm gives a comprehensive view of the relation of the creature to the creator.

XIV. Psalm 149

This psalm breathes the spirit of intense joy and eager hope which must have been characteristic of the period succeeding the return from captivity in Babylon. Men of strong faith, religious enthusiasm and fervent loyalty must have felt that the restoration to their own land was a signal, or proof, of divine favor. The restoration could only be regarded as a pledge of a glorious picture yet in store for the nation.

XV. Psalm 150

This is the great closing doxology of the Book of Psalms or Psalter. In this hallelujah, every kind of musical instrument was to have its part as well as the voice of man. Not just one nation only, but "everything that hath breath" was invited to join.

The last three psalms ascended from praise to higher praise until, in Psalm 150, there is unlimited exultation which knows no bounds. The joy overflows and spreads throughout the universe. Every creature joins the praise chorus. Heaven is full of praise; the earth is full of praise. It is as though the soul gave utterance of its whole life and feeling in one word, Hallelujah! "Praise Him" is repeated no less than nine times in this psalm of six short verses.

"Praise the Lord!" — "Praise God!" — "Praise Him!"

Daily Bible Study Questions for Group Discussion

Note: Read notes and Scripture references before answering the questions. Some questions are for those more advanced in Bible Study. Try to answer all questions but don't be discouraged if some seem a little hard. Unless otherwise instructed, use Bible only in answering questions.

(Next week your questions will be review, mix and match, true and false, matching, fill in and brain teasers. Some will be a challenge. Following discussion group time, there will be an introduction to the Book of Proverbs.)

FIRST DAY: Read notes on Lesson 24.

1. From your notes, what are some of the losses the Jews experienced as a result of their apostasy?

2. You have heard it said, "You can take a boy from the farm but you can't take the farm from the boy." How would this concept somewhat apply to the children of Israel in Babylon?

3. Which psalm in this lesson emphasized the attributes of God?

4. Of all the psalms in this lesson, which was the most meaningful to you personally and why?

5. Although this series of psalms are for praise, they also include verses of prayers by the psalmist. Which of these prayers would be good and meaningful for us to include in our daily prayer? Give psalm and verses.

SECOND DAY: Review question.

Psalm 46:1	Psalm 139:23-24	Psalm 23:6
Psalm 19:1	Psalm 18:30	Psalm 46:10
Psalm 1:1	Psalm 119:11	Psalm 18:2
Psalm 55:22	Psalm 19:14	Psalm 37:4
Psalm 118:24	Psalm 62:2	Psalm 11:3

6. **Mix and Match.** Match references above with the text below.

_____ a. *"If the foundations are destroyed, what can the righteous do?"*

_____ b. *"Blessed is the man who walks not in the counsel of the ungodly, nor stands in the path of sinners, Nor sits in the seat of the scornful."*

_____ c. *"The Lord is my rock and my fortress and my deliverer; my God, my strength, in whom I will trust; my shield and the horn of my salvation, my stronghold."*

_____ d. *"As for God, His way is perfect; the word of the Lord is proven; He is a shield to all who trust in Him."*

_____ e. *"The heavens declare the glory of God; and the firmament shows His handiwork."*

_____ f. *"Let the words of my mouth and the meditation of my heart be acceptable in Your sight, O Lord, my strength and my Redeemer."*

_____ g. *"Surely goodness and mercy shall follow me all the days of my life; and I will dwell in the house of the Lord forever."*

_____ h. *"Delight yourself also in the Lord, and He shall give you the desires of your heart."*

_____ i. *"God is our refuge and strength, a very present help in trouble."*

_____ j. *"Be still, and know that I am God; I will be exalted among the nations, I will be exalted in the earth!"*

_____ k. *"Cast your burden on the Lord, and He shall sustain you; He shall never permit the righteous to be moved."*

_____ l. *"He only is my rock and my salvation; He is my defense; I shall not be greatly moved."*

_____ m. *"This is the day the Lord has made; we will rejoice and be glad in it."*

_____ n. *"Your word I have hidden in my heart, that I might not sin against You!"*

_____ o. *"Search me, O God, and know my heart; try me, and know my anxieties; and see if there is any wicked way in me, and lead me in the way everlasting."*

THIRD DAY:

7. **True and False.**

_____ a. The children of Israel spent forty years in captivity because of disobedience to God.

_____ b. The enemies of God were also the enemy of the Israelites.

_____ c. David's son Solomon tried to usurp the throne of his father David.

_____ d. In their land of captivity the Israelites soon forgot their homeland and integrated into the religion and customs of Babylon.

_____ e. Psalm 119 is the longest Psalm in the Book of Psalms.

_____ f. David twice had to flee Jerusalem because of Saul then his son Absalom.

_____ g. Jerusalem is also called Zion, the city of God.

_____ h. The wicked do not prosper. Only those who put their trust in God can expect to be successful.

_____ i. The penitential prayer of David for his awful sin of the flesh is found in Psalm 62.

_____ j. The shortest Psalm is 134.

_____ k. The Psalms have much to say about the Word and reasons for studying, memorizing and living according to its precepts and principles.

_____ l. The Psalms teach us that God is the source of all we need if we will but put our trust in Him.

FOURTH DAY:

8. **Fill in the blanks.**

    a. "I will _____ You, O Lord, with my _____ heart; I will tell of all Your _____ works."

    b. "The _____ has said in his heart, '____ ___ ___ _____.' They are corrupt, they have done _____ works, there is none who does good."

    c. "You will show me the _____ _____ _____; In Your _____ is _____ of ____; at Your right hand are p_____ forevermore."

    d. "He only is my _____ and my _____; He is my _____; I shall not be greatly moved."

    e. "Blessed be the Lord, who _____ loads us with _____, the God of our _____ ."

    f. "In the day of my _____ I will call upon You, for You will _____ me."

    g. "_____ me Your way, O Lord; I will _____ in Your _____; unite my _____ to fear Your _____ ."

    h. "So _____ us to _____ our days, That we may _____ a heart of _____ ."

    i. "He who d_____ in the _____ place of the Most High shall _____ under the _____ of the _____ ."

Psalm 90:12	Psalm 9:1	Psalm 91:1
Psalm 86:11	Psalm 86:7	Psalm 14:1
Psalm 68:19	Psalm 16:11	Psalm 62:2

FIFTH DAY: Essay.

9. Sit down and take a little time to think about your past weeks of study. Write a few short sentences of what this study has meant to you. What would you have to tell someone else about your study?

SIXTH DAY:

10. **Unscramble the words and match.**

a.	venhea	comfort
b.	tesnerssghiou	justice
c.	ctusanary	rejoice
d.	sinblesg	worship
e.	ispwroh	quicken
f.	oomfcrt	prayer
g.	kenquic	blessing
h.	timtesyon	peace
i.	ustjice	faithfulness
j.	remcy	sanctuary
k.	flafihtu	unsearchable
l.	icerejo	testimony
m.	eceap	righteousness
n.	gndessnkinlovi	everlasting
o.	lsatngierev	mercy
p.	bemerrem	thanksgiving
q.	yraper	heaven
r.	fhlussenaitf	faithful
s.	usacalebhren	remember
t.	ksiviganhtng	lovingkindness

Notes

Notes

Book of Proverbs

Introduction

The Proverbs of Solomon are a collection of wise sayings. This collection was known as the Book of Wisdom by early Christian writers and is still referred to as such in some translations of the Bible.

Solomon was the son of David, and his successor to the throne of Israel. The Jewish writers place the Book of Proverbs as having been written during the middle life of King Solomon. This would have been about two hundred and sixty years before the reign of Cyrus. King Solomon wrote the book of Proverbs with the exception of Chapters 30 and 31. Chapter 30 was written by Agur and Chapter 31 was written by King Lemuel and his mother.

The Book of Proverbs includes both moral sentences and proverbs. A proverb is a short moral sentence, but it is distinctive in that the words mean something other than that which they naturally and literally imply. *"Trust in the Lord with all your heart, and lean not on your own understanding"* (Proverbs 3:5) is not a proverb, it is a moral sentence. *"Drink water from your own cistern"* (Proverbs 5:15), is a proverb because the moral is expressed in a figurative manner. The meaning is that one should not meddle with that which belongs to another. *"A wise son makes a glad father, but a foolish son is the grief of his mother."* (Proverbs 10:1). The first half of this proverb describes the wise son; the second, the foolish. The joy of the father is set over against the grief of the mother in the second part, and the contrast heightens its force. Proverbs 10:8 is another example: *"The wise in heart will receive commands, but a prating fool will fall."* There is a double contrast: (1) The wise hearted man (instead of prating perpetually himself) hears and receives advice; while the fool prates with deaf ears. (2) The wise man (it is implied) lives and prospers by means of wise counsels which he both hears and obeys; while the prating fool neither hearing

nor heeding counsel, falls into ruin. The secondary contrast lies between what is affirmed of the fool and what is left inferred of the wise. (Note: Prating is to talk much and long to little purpose; foolish or empty talk.) In comparison, a proverb would be *"As vinegar to the teeth and smoke to the eyes, so is the lazy man to those who send him"* (Proverbs 10:26). Another example is (Proverbs 10:25). *"When the whirlwind passes by, the wicked is no more, but the righteous has an everlasting foundation."* The passing away of the wicked is compared to a whirlwind, with the contrast of the enduring life and blessedness of the righteous.

Solomon was inspired to use his wisdom and acquired knowledge to interpret the lessons of his own wide experience in writing wise, practical counsels for all that should live after him. He did this in brief sentences, using either the proverb, a figurative form of expression, or by plain statement. His purpose was to set forth the principles and rules of right living in this world. His themes include almost every topic touching personal and social relations, rights and duties, happiness and success of the individual, the family and the community. It is a manual of ethics or right conduct. For the individual, it furnishes all essential counsels pertaining to sobriety, purity and all honesty or integrity, as well as to industry and economy. Samuel T. Coleridge says, "It is the best statesman's manual that was ever written. An adherence to the political economy and spirit of that collection of concise sayings and essays would do more to eradicate the causes of extravagance, corruption, and ruin if people would heed these words of advice. Though civilization changes, though customs differ, yet man's nature and conduct are the same in every age and among all people. Therefore, these sayings in Proverbs sum up principles of right living in positive counsel or the negative one of warning. They always have a universal application." Although not always directly having distinctive Christian instruction, its guidance is always in harmony with New Testament teaching. The Book of Proverbs teaches many subjects not fully developed in the New Testament, and helps in guiding us into the way of wisdom.

There is no book more useful to us for devotions than that of David's Psalms, and no book is more serviceable to us for the right ordering of our conversation as Solomon's Proverbs. There is a vast collection of sayings in Proverbs relating to life, duty, the fear of God, charity to man, modesty, humility, forbearance, industry and self-denial. Here we see that one plain use and design of the whole book is to give us a quantity of short expressions of deep truths that we can carry with us and call to mind when we need them.

The content of this book will imprint upon our minds the great truths of God's providence and the penetrating understanding of God's judgment.

It is impossible for anyone to read the Book of Proverbs without profit. It is distinguishable from the writings of the Prophets and the Psalms. One author describes the content of Proverbs as having something of a worldly prudent manner, unlike the rest of the Bible. But this is the very reason why its recognition as a sacred book is so useful. It is the philosophy of practical life. It impresses upon us the value of intelligence and prudence, and of a good education. It also deals in that refined, discriminating, careful view, the shades of human character which are necessary to any true estimate of human life. *"The heart knows its own bitterness, and a stranger does not share its joy"* (Proverbs 14:10). Above all, it repeatedly states the doctrine that goodness is "wisdom" and that wickedness and vice are "folly." Although there may be other views of virtue and vice, of holiness and sin that are higher and better than this, there will always be some in the world who will need to remember that a good man is not only religious and just, but wise; and that a bad man is not only wicked and sinful, but desolate.

The same human tendencies exist among us today as existed in Solomon's day. The same passions are seen at work; the same desires; the same strength and the same weaknesses of virtue. We can observe

the greed of gain which brought about ruin and death and the search for wisdom being neglected for the making of money. Nothing was allowed to stand in the way. In spite of starving people, dealers withheld their corn from sale till financial gains rewarded them. This was contrary to the spirit of Hebrew law. False balances and unjust weights were common. The hope of gain outweighed the loss which was sure to follow. The pursuit of wealth was the fruitful mother of selfishness and wrong doing.

The extensive commerce of Solomon's reign presented chances of honorably realizing great riches. *"In all labor there is profit"* says Solomon, correctly laying down the first principle of our political economy; *"but idle chatter leads only to poverty"* (Proverbs 14:23). A mere talker was contemptible in Solomon's sight. A true worker was one who profited by honest labor. *"The crown of the wise is their riches"* (Proverbs 14:24).

Rulers and judges indulged in wine and strong drink. Drunkenness had become common. The drunkard is compared to a voyager on a stormy sea, who chooses for his bed the unsteady top of a mast in a swaying ship. A graphic picture is given of the helpless drunkard, muttering incoherent thoughts to himself. *"Who has woe? Who has sorrow? Who has contentions? Who has complaints? Who has wounds without cause? Who has redness of eyes? Those who linger long at the wine, those who go in search of mixed wine"* (Proverbs 23:29-30).

Indecent women seem to have been common in the cities of Palestine. It does not say that they were Hebrew women. A vast number of heathen were in the king's service and were transported to the Lebanon woods. Many women must have been left destitute and friendless. Indecency, which was the curse of Solomon's large cities, may have been the result of a shifting population. Honest women were the fairest ornament and stronghold of the land. Nothing is more striking in the Book of Proverbs than the contrast between the decent woman and the indecent woman. Shame and ruin of the one; wealth and honor the other. Deceit and treachery were waiting at street corners to snare the young man. Honorable marriage and vows honorably kept enabled thrifty women to place their husbands among the rulers of the land, to clothe all their household in scarlet, and to fill their houses with every good thing. A virtuous wife is compared to *"the merchant ships, she brings her food from afar"* (Proverbs 31:14).

What men and women strive for today in various duties and labors of life is much the same as in the days of Solomon. Circumstances have not changed, but experience has added many examples to confirm the consequences of the choice of life- styles. Solomon's proverbial philosophy, *"The fear of the Lord is a fountain of life, to turn one away from the snares of death"* (Proverbs 14:27).

This is especially a book for the young. Often we read the words, "My son," because young men are most vulnerable to the sins that destroy character and make life bitter. They are particularly warned against four sins — impurity, intemperance, lying and robbery. The warnings against impurity of life are the most frequent. Regarding wickedness, Solomon describes the subtlety of temptations, the suddenness of the fall, the bitterness of the awakening, and the inevitable and long life of remorse. The man who loses his virtue through sexual sins takes a viper into his heart. He will always hear the hissing and feel the sting.

There is also the sin of intemperance, warning youth who would be tempted by the color of the wine and deceived by the temporary excitement that proves injurious to mind, soul, and body. Solomon's advice is total abstinence. His advice represents the sober judgment of every age. He speaks to the young as a critical group, whose power of body and mind are still in the process of development. To them, he says what every concerned lover of the young must still say, "Let the wine cup alone." *"Wine is a mocker, strong drink is a brawler, and whoever is led astray by it is not wise"* (Proverbs 20:1).

Solomon then strongly advises the young against every form of lying and slander. A man's word must be as good as his bond. Modern commercial life is one grand exhibition of fidelity to trusts. Don't lie in word or conduct. Finally, Solomon warns the young against robbery of every kind, whether it be the robbery of violence or the robbery of false weights and measures. Don't steal. Three feet to the yard; sixteen ounces to the pound; a fair equivalent to every bargain you make — this is Solomon's advice. Solomon was a great merchant as well as a king.

This book is full of good common sense and is the best practical guide for young men today. Five great positive virtues are commended to the young man who values an honorable ambition and these are: a regard for parental advice, industry, economy, contentment and piety. Sluggishness invites disaster. Laziness and wastefulness are great enemies of prosperity.

The Proverbs of Solomon are in three divisions:

1. Chapters 1-9 are addressed to the young.
2. Chapters 10-24 are addressed to all ages.
3. Chapters 25-29 are a later collection made by scribes under Hezekiah from records of the wisdom of Solomon.

There are two added appendices. Chapter thirty contains the words of Agur. They are called his "prophecy". Nothing is known of this writer. The thirty-first chapter are the words of Lemuel, the king, who possibly could have been an Arab prince.

Daily Bible Study Questions for Group Discussion

Note: Read notes and Scripture references before answering the questions. Some questions are for those more advanced in Bible Study. Try to answer all questions but don't be discouraged if some seem a little hard. Unless otherwise instructed, use Bible only in answering questions.

FIRST DAY: Read notes for Lesson #25.

    1.   What is a Proverb?

    2.   What is another title used for the Book of Proverbs?

    3.   About what time in the life of Solomon do the Jewish writers contribute the writing of the Book of Proverbs?

    4.   What was Solomon's purpose in writing the Proverbs?

SECOND DAY:

    5.   What are some of the general topics covered in the Book of Proverbs?

    6.   Though many things do change, what two things remain the same in all people and through the ages of time?

7. a) Of which four sins are the young particularly warned?

    b) Why?

THIRD DAY: Read Proverbs 1.

8. After considering **verses 1-6**, what are your personal expectations from studying the Book of Proverbs?

9. In this chapter there is a contrast with the call of wisdom and the enticement of sinners. What are the results of accepting or rejecting wisdom?

10. **Read verses 22 - 33**, regarding the Jews and their rejection of our Lord Jesus Christ. Considering the fact they had the Old Testament Scripture, what in these verses helps us to know their problem?

FOURTH DAY: Read Proverbs 2-3.

11. In these chapters underline in your Bible or on your text work sheet the directions given for the attaining of wisdom.

12. (a) With a different colored pencil underline on your text work sheet benefits which wisdom brings.

    (b) With another colored pencil on your text work sheet, underline the evils that wisdom protects us from.

13. **Read Hebrews 12:5-10**. What importance does the writer of Hebrews give to the words "My Son"?

FIFTH AND SIXTH DAYS: Read Proverbs 4-5.

14. What outstanding lessons in these chapters does the speaker want to impress upon us? Here again, if you choose, mark your Bibles or text work sheet.

15. What words of warning are given to follow the counsel?

16. **Chapter 4:23-27** gives a guide to successful living. What direction is given concerning the heart, lips, eyes and feet?

Proverbs 2

2:1 My son, if you receive my words, And treasure my commands within you,

2 So that you incline your ear to wisdom, And apply your heart to understanding;

3 Yes, if you cry out for discernment, And lift up your voice for understanding,

4 If you seek her as silver, And search for her as for hidden treasures;

5 Then you will understand the fear of the LORD, And find the knowledge of God.

6 For the LORD gives wisdom; From His mouth come knowledge and understanding;

7 He stores up sound wisdom for the upright; He is a shield to those who walk uprightly;

8 He guards the paths of justice, And preserves the way of His saints.

9 Then you will understand righteousness and justice, Equity and every good path.

10 When wisdom enters your heart, And knowledge is pleasant to your soul,

11 Discretion will preserve you; Understanding will keep you,

12 To deliver you from the way of evil, From the man who speaks perverse things,

13 From those who leave the paths of uprightness To walk in the ways of darkness;

14 Who rejoice in doing evil, And delight in the perversity of the wicked;

15 Whose ways are crooked, And who are devious in their paths;

16 To deliver you from the immoral woman, From the seductress who flatters with her words,

17 Who forsakes the companion of her youth, And forgets the covenant of her God.

18 For her house leads down to death, And her paths to the dead;

19 None who go to her return, Nor do they regain the paths of life;

20 So you may walk in the way of goodness, And keep to the paths of righteousness.

21 For the upright will dwell in the land, And the blameless will remain in it;

22 But the wicked will be cut off from the earth, And the unfaithful will be uprooted from it.

Proverbs 3

3:1 My son, do not forget my law, But let your heart keep my commands;

2 For length of days and long life And peace they will add to you.

3 Let not mercy and truth forsake you; Bind them around your neck, Write them on the tablet of your heart,

4 And so find favor and high esteem In the sight of God and man.

5 Trust in the LORD with all your heart, And lean not on your own understanding;6 In all your ways acknowledge Him, And He shall direct your paths.

7 Do not be wise in your own eyes; Fear the LORD and depart from evil.

8 It will be health to your flesh, And strength to your bones.

9 Honor the LORD with your possessions, And with the firstfruits of all your increase;

10 So your barns will be filled with plenty, And your vats will overflow with new wine.

11 My son, do not despise the chastening of the LORD, Nor detest His correction;

12 For whom the LORD loves He corrects, Just as a father the son in whom he delights.

13 Happy is the man who finds wisdom, And the man who gains understanding;

14 For her proceeds are better than the profits of silver, And her gain than fine gold.

15 She is more precious than rubies, And all the things you may desire cannot compare with her.

16 Length of days is in her right hand, In her left hand riches and honor.

17 Her ways are ways of pleasantness, And all her paths are peace.

18 She is a tree of life to those who take hold of her, And happy are all who retain her.

19 The LORD by wisdom founded the earth; By understanding He established the heavens;

20 By His knowledge the depths were broken up, And clouds drop down the dew.

21 My son, let them not depart from your eyes; Keep sound wisdom and discretion;

22 So they will be life to your soul And grace to your neck.

23 Then you will walk safely in your way, And your foot will not stumble.

24 When you lie down, you will not be afraid; Yes, you will lie down and your sleep will be sweet.

25 Do not be afraid of sudden terror, Nor of trouble from the wicked when it comes;

26 For the LORD will be your confidence, And will keep your foot from being caught.

27 Do not withhold good from those to whom it is due, When it is in the power of your hand to do so.

28 Do not say to your neighbor, "Go, and come back, And tomorrow I will give it," When you have it with you.

29 Do not devise evil against your neighbor, For he dwells by you for safety's sake.

30 Do not strive with a man without cause, If he has done you no harm.

31 Do not envy the oppressor, And choose none of his ways;

32 For the perverse person is an abomination to the LORD, But His secret counsel is with the upright.

33 The curse of the LORD is on the house of the wicked, But He blesses the home of the just.

34 Surely He scorns the scornful, But gives grace to the humble.

35 The wise shall inherit glory, But shame shall be the legacy of fools.

Proverbs 4

4:1 Hear, my children, the instruction of a father, And give attention to know understanding;

2 For I give you good doctrine: Do not forsake my law.

3 When I was my father's son, Tender and the only one in the sight of my mother,

4 He also taught me, and said to me: "Let your heart retain my words; Keep my commands, and live.

5 Get wisdom! Get understanding! Do not forget, nor turn away from the words of my mouth.

6 Do not forsake her, and she will preserve you; Love her, and she will keep you.

7 Wisdom is the principal thing; Therefore get wisdom. And in all your getting, get understanding.

8 Exalt her, and she will promote you; She will bring you honor, when you embrace her.

9 She will place on your head an ornament of grace; A crown of glory she will deliver to you."

10 Hear, my son, and receive my sayings, And the years of your life will be many.

11 I have taught you in the way of wisdom; I have led you in right paths.

12 When you walk, your steps will not be hindered, And when you run, you will not stumble.

13 Take firm hold of instruction, do not let go; Keep her, for she is your life.

14 Do not enter the path of the wicked, And do not walk in the way of evil.

15 Avoid it, do not travel on it; Turn away from it and pass on.

16 For they do not sleep unless they have done evil; And their sleep is taken away unless they make someone fall.

17 For they eat the bread of wickedness, And drink the wine of violence.

18 But the path of the just is like the shining sun, That shines ever brighter unto the perfect day.

19 The way of the wicked is like darkness; They do not know what makes them stumble.

20 My son, give attention to my words; Incline your ear to my sayings.

21 Do not let them depart from your eyes; Keep them in the midst of your heart;

22 For they are life to those who find them, And health to all their flesh.

23 Keep your heart with all diligence, For out of it spring the issues of life.

24 Put away from you a deceitful mouth, And put perverse lips far from you.

25 Let your eyes look straight ahead, And your eyelids look right before you.

26 Ponder the path of your feet, And let all your ways be established.

27 Do not turn to the right or the left; Remove your foot from evil.

Proverbs 5

5:1 My son, pay attention to my wisdom; Lend your ear to my understanding,

2 That you may preserve discretion, And your lips may keep knowledge.

3 For the lips of an immoral woman drip honey, And her mouth is smoother than oil;

4 But in the end she is bitter as wormwood, Sharp as a two-edged sword.

5 Her feet go down to death, Her steps lay hold of hell.

6 Lest you ponder her path of life; Her ways are unstable; You do not know them.

7 Therefore hear me now, my children, And do not depart from the words of my mouth.

8 Remove your way far from her, And do not go near the door of her house,

9 Lest you give your honor to others, And your years to the cruel one;

10 Lest aliens be filled with your wealth, And your labors go to the house of a foreigner;

11 And you mourn at last, When your flesh and your body are consumed,

12 And say: "How I have hated instruction, And my heart despised correction!

13 I have not obeyed the voice of my teachers, Nor inclined my ear to those who instructed me!

14 I was on the verge of total ruin, In the midst of the assembly and congregation."

15 Drink water from your own cistern, And running water from your own well.

16 Should your fountains be dispersed abroad, Streams of water in the streets?

17 Let them be only your own, And not for strangers with you.

18 Let your fountain be blessed, And rejoice with the wife of your youth.

19 As a loving deer and a graceful doe, Let her breasts satisfy you at all times; And always be enraptured with her love.

20 For why should you, my son, be enraptured by an immoral woman, And be embraced in the arms of a seductress?

21 For the ways of man are before the eyes of the LORD, And He ponders all his paths.

22 His own iniquities entrap the wicked man, And he is caught in the cords of his sin.

23 He shall die for lack of instruction, And in the greatness of his folly he shall go astray.

Notes

Notes

Proverbs 1-5

I. Proverbs 1

A. Introduction (Proverbs 1:1-7)

The author began his book of Proverbs by giving a clear statement of purpose for writing the book: to give understanding or knowledge of wisdom, to give useful instruction, to give proper teaching on morality and to settle questions of right and wrong. A careful reading of the Book of Proverbs will provide instruction and true moral and spiritual wisdom. For those who genuinely desire "to know wisdom," Proverbs is the key that unlocks the door.

This Book of Proverbs will be found useful to the simple and young. The word "prudence" is used in the sense of sharp and clear discrimination. The "simple" refers to the open-hearted and unsuspecting who are susceptible to social influence and easily receive impressions for good or evil. The "young" are those whose age places them in a category of being easily influenced. They need both knowledge and discipline. Youth is the time to learn truth and a time in which opinions are formed. It is crucial for them to learn truth so that they will be spiritually discerning.

"A wise man will hear and increase learning" (verse 5). True wisdom is always progressing. What is learned in the past and present is always a basis for further advances. The *"fear of the Lord"* (verse 7) is a reverential relationship in which the love for God blends with a respect to God and rises to the highest reverence. It is then that we desire above all else to learn and do His will. This *"fear of the Lord"* is vital to the acquisition of all true wisdom so that it may be said that this is the very beginning of wisdom. It is the starting point. It is not found in keen insight, nor experience, nor education, but in the spirit of reverence and awe. This fear has no torment, for it is compatible with love. The knowledge of God is the perfection of love.

B. Warning Against Evil Companions (Proverbs 1:8-19)

In these verses, instruction begins with an exhortation to obedience to both father and mother. In the Ten Commandments, we are admonished to *"Honor your father and your mother, that your days may be long upon the land which the Lord your God is giving you"* (Exodus 20:12). This commandment is also taught in the New Testament. Ephesians 6:1-3 says, *"Children, obey your parents in the Lord, for this is right. Honor your father and mother, etc. . . . ."* This is the first commandment with a promise. Disobedience to parents today is an indication of the last days. If children are disobedient to parents, they will be disobedient to God. Disobedience is a root cause of ungodliness. The admonition for respect and obedience to parents is followed by a warning against associating with wicked companions. These are lawless and desperate people, thieves and murderers who are greedy for gain. The young person is warned not to walk in the way with them. Sinners love company and they entice and flatter in order to draw the young person into their net. Wickedness is human selfishness which recklessly plays its games upon others' interests and rights. Often the wicked slip by the law and it is the one who really never intended to get entangled in a net of robbery and murder who gets caught and pays the penalty. So Solomon admonishes: *"keep your foot from their path."* Young people must remember the word "Resist." It takes courage and character and one who resists may not be popular with those who entice youth into sin, but there is victory in winning this battle. Those who corrupt are the weak and cowardly.

C. The Appeal to Wisdom (Proverbs 1:20-33)

The allurements to evil in the world and the consequences of yielding to tempters, referred to in the proceeding verses, suggest the call of a heavenly

One. Throughout the Book of Proverbs, wisdom represents piety or godlikeness of heart and life. It is opposed to foolish actions. Christ is the only manifested embodiment of this exalted idea of wisdom. His Spirit perfectly harmonizes with this personified messenger of God to man. His office and work, both in word and deed, correspond exactly with that indicated in this Divine message. Therefore, it is a natural and necessary conclusion that Christ Himself is represented here. The New Testament confirms this conclusion. Keep in mind this reference to Christ in the personified wisdom of the proverbs and notice the interchangeable use of the abstract idea of loyalty or religion with the personal Christ. Observe the openness and universality of this call to men. Openly travelling every pathway of man and seeking out all classes, this herald of heaven is represented as crying aloud to the multitudes gathered in the gateways and other places of travel and to those abiding in their homes.

In verses 22-23, three classes of people are mentioned: The **simple** or the unsuspecting or inexperienced that are easily ensnared and led into evil by worldly tempters and enticement; the **scorner**, a man who despises truth; a scoffer of God and religion. In the third class, scorning has deepened into hate of the truth and of God. **Fools** identify men that openly defy God and are self-abandoned to their lusts. The first psalm mentions the same three classes. The same gradation of character is also indicated by the attitudes of walking, standing and sitting. The call comes: *"Turn at my rebuke"* (Proverbs 1:23). The meaning is 'Repent and become wise.' Then follows the promise of the Spirit and the Word of God. There is opportunity for the sinner to turn to God.

"Because I have called and you refused" (Proverbs 1:24). Christ has stretched forth His hands, but ye have refused, despised and rejected My counsels and promises. All that remains is a strong warning: *"My Spirit shall not strive with man forever"* (Genesis 6:3). How unwise not to respond to the call of the Master. Not responding, they shall reap as they have sown; misery for sin, remorse and despair and hardness of heart. *"Do not be deceived, God is not mocked; for whatever a man sows, that he will also reap. For he who sows to his flesh will of the flesh reap corruption, but he who sows to* the Spirit will of the Spirit reap everlasting life" (Galatians 6:7-8).

II. Proverbs 2
A. The Results of Pursuing Wisdom (Proverbs 2:1-9)

A sincere disciple must first receive and then lay up or carefully keep the Words, therefore placing value on His instructions. Earthly wisdom is gained by study, heavenly wisdom by prayer. Study makes one a Biblical scholar; prayer forms the wise and spiritual Christian. Let prayer give life and energy to your study. Believe God for true wisdom and He will teach you more and more. *"If you seek her* (wisdom) *as silver, and search for her as for hidden treasures; then you will understand"* (Proverbs 2:4-5). Jewels do not lie on the surface of the ground, but they are hid in the earth. You must dig for them before you can enjoy them. You must search for the truth of God as for hid treasure. Wisdom is referred to as something you must labor for. The search is to be the business of a person's life. There are enough lessons in God's Word for every day of the longest life. You can never exhaust your study of the living Word. For the serious student it demands patient and persevering study. The writer of Hebrews warns, *"Therefore we must give the more earnest heed to the things we have heard, lest we drift away."* (Hebrews 2:1) This is a warning to Christians who do not continually study God's Word. God holds man responsible for his belief. He has given us His Word and we choose to believe that God means what He says or to ignore it partially or wholly. Because we choose to ignore it does not mean that we will not be held responsible and accountable to God for its content. His Word is our guidebook for life. We need to study it for direction. Men will guard their **opinions** almost with their life. How much more important it is to guard the truth of God's Word. Our belief should be based on that alone. It is through His Word that we understand the fear of the Lord and find knowledge.

"If any of you lacks wisdom, let him ask of God, who gives to all liberally and without reproach, and it will be given to him" (James 1:5). One can believe the Bible only so far as he has appropriated Biblical truths in his life. There is truth above us which is our master, there is a law over us which we are to obey; but that truth and that law

are also to be in us, so that they become our truth and our law. Christian truth and Christian faith exist only for those to whom they become a personal possession and a living power.

B. Being Kept From the Evil Man and the Strange Woman (Proverbs 2:10-19)

When wisdom enters the heart there is rejoicing in true knowledge. The consequences that follow are preservation and deliverance. The ways of the evil man holds no attraction for those who love and seek wisdom. The text takes a new direction from verses 16 to 22. We have studied the blessings of wisdom and knowledge, of guidance and protection, and deliverance from evil. Now the writer deals with one special evil, that of lacking restraint especially in our sexual appetite. True wisdom will deliver those who possess restraint from the defiling and destructive results of promiscuous sexual behavior. The fact that it mentions in verse 17 *"the covenant of her God,"* seems to relate that this strange woman is a Jewish woman who has taken on the practice of prostitution as was common among Cannanitish women. *"The covenant of her God"* indicates that in the ceremony of marriage at that time, appeal was made to God, who was called to witness the vows and promises made. The adulterous woman broke the vows of this covenant. She had a double load of guilt: that which respects her husband and that which has respect to her God. A man can be marred or ruined for life by falling into the trap of an unchaste woman. We can see modern examples of this to help us understand the consequences. The sentiment of verse 18 is *"For her house leads down to death, and her paths to the dead."* This is a warning particularly to youth who may be enticed by an adulteress. Both she and her house sink down bodily into the open jaws of hell. They sink into the realms of the lost. All who go into her house for such guilty purposes never return again to take hold of the paths of the life of purity. In the Mosaic law the crime of being an adulteress was thought to be so serious that it was punishable with death (Deuteronomy 22:22-24). Today our civil laws are less stern but God still hates the sins of the flesh. Only those who have been entrapped fully know the sad consequences.

III. Proverbs 3

A. The Call and Promise of Wisdom (Proverbs 3:1-10)

Solomon details the best policy for attaining success in the first ten verses of this chapter. This is his instruction: Observe God's commands, particularly the practice of kindness and faithful dealings with men; a self forgetting trust in God and thankful recognition of His every gift; a fear of God that restrains from evil; a consecration of earthly substance; an habitual giving of tithe of all substance and an understanding of trials as part of God's training. The promises or reasons for following these directions are these: the possession and enjoyment of a long and peaceful life, of the favor of God and man, of divine guidance in every plan, of spiritual health, abundant success in our labor and our returning to God both of ourselves and our substance that which belongs to Him (verse 9). God has promised to bless the liberal and cheerful giver. Giving cheerfully, liberally, habitually and gratefully, as unto the Lord, has served to work wonders in the hearts and lives of God's people. *"It is more blessed to give than to receive"* (Acts 20:35).

B. Happy is the Man That Findeth Wisdom (Proverbs 3:11-20)

These verses appropriately follow promises of blessing. The trustful and obedient, regardless of prosperity, will encounter adversity. Sickness and pain, disappointment and sorrow, change and bereavement belong to every human experience. They are the familiar instruments by which the Lord chastens and are used by Him in the highest interest of His children. We must honor God by rightly interpreting them, by submissively accepting their purpose, *"For whom the Lord loves He corrects"* (Proverbs 3:12).

Chastisement is not a pleasant word as we generally associate it with displeasure and severity on the part of the one who administers it. Chastisement in its root sense is correction as a means of improvement. It is instruction, guidance and training. It represents the love and work of the father, the teacher, the trainer and the guide. It makes a difference as to whether we look on our affliction as chastisement or as the loving Father who is proving His love by the chastisement. If we look at the chastening, it seems to be *"not joyous, but grievous."* If we look at God as our loving Father, we can be sure that whatever He sends to us is the best for us. His chastenings are to be welcomed as a proof of His affection. In verses 13-18 the worth of wisdom and its value is rated by comparison with worldly success, treasures, and delights. The one who finds wisdom and holds it dear is happy. Wisdom needs to be sought for, found and kept. It is as a precious jewel. Wisdom stands before us with the blessings she has to bestow. Long life in one hand; in the other riches and honor; her ways are pleasantness and her paths are peace. A "tree of life" is a perennial fountain of good, worthy to represent the joys of heaven. These verses are descriptive of the blessedness of wisdom, and have been greatly loved for their richness and beauty. The wisdom that begins in the fear and love of God, and accepted as the guiding hand of the All-wise Father, is a fountain of perpetual blessedness. Wisdom's ways always have one fixed mark or goal, and that goal is the glory of God.

C. Promise and Instruction
(Proverbs 3:21-35)

The teacher continues admonishing his pupil, persuading him to cleave to the pursuit of wisdom. It will keep him in safety; he may lie down in security and sleep sweetly, no fear of destruction will disturb him because God is his Keeper (verses 21 - 26). The following five verses are prohibitions. One must not withhold good from his neighbor; he must not put off a favor to him which he can do now; he must not slander him; he must not contend with him without cause and he must not be envious of an oppressor nor choose his ways (verses 27-31). God is the Friend of the righteous; His curse is on the house of the wicked, and the dwelling of the just is blessed (verses 32-33). He mocks the scorners, and shows favor to the righteous, the wise shall inherit glory, but shame shall take away fools (verses 34, 35). (Paraphrased)

IV. Proverbs 4

A. The Loving Instruction of a Father
(Proverbs 4:1-9)

The youth are exhorted to listen to wise and good instruction. The writer says that as a child he had received loving parental instruction and that youth

should hear and obey diligently. He was to acquire wisdom and never deviate from it so that he would be kept safe from evil. Wisdom is the first priority, then understanding should be pursued with all diligence. The promise is: She shall preserve thee; she shall keep thee; she shall promote thee; she gives honor; and an ornament of grace for the head and a crown of glory.

B. Son, Receive My Sayings
(Proverbs 4:10-19)

"Take firm hold of instruction, do not let go; keep her, for she is your life" (verse 13). Life means not just living in the world with minimum comfort. It is not just having enough bread to eat to keep us from hunger or enough to wear to keep us warm. Life means growing into the image of Christ Himself. A Christian's desire should be to grow into a strong, well disciplined character and into a blessed peace with God. If we expect to receive all God has for us, we are not to enter the wrong path but choose the definite and positive right way. The wrong way is to be avoided; *"Avoid it, do not travel on it; turn away from it and pass on"* (verse 15). This applies to all forms and degrees of evil doing. I believe one of our problems today is that we have lost a sense of what is evil and become apathetic. Things which once were considered sin have been approved by the general consensus of society and people who profess to be Christians have seemingly lost discernment as to what God approves and what He doesn't approve. The root cause of this is that we don't know what the Bible teaches. We are going to be judged by the Word. How important it is to know it! Modern day media makes sin common and it becomes easy to lose our sensitivity to it. Unless our young people are instructed in the Word we cannot expect anything other than the sad consequences we are experiencing. Ours is a broken and sick society and we should be challenged to share with others the only solution — God's Word and a commitment to Christ.

C. My Son, attend to My words
(Proverbs 4:20-27)

These verses give instruction to receive and to obey the words of wisdom. The eye is never to be taken from the words of the Lord. His words are to be kept in the midst of the heart.

V.   Proverbs 5

A. Shun the Strange Woman and Sinful Passion (Proverbs 5:1-14)

This chapter deals with adultery. The strange woman entices with flattery which results in bitter and destructive consequences. Her steps go down to hell. A strong warning is emphasized again in verses 7 to 10 to keep far from the way of the strange woman and from the door of her house. In other words, in no way be identified with harlots, prostitutes or adulteresses. Many have had their reputation ruined by the appearances of association with someone of ill-repute. Bitter sorrows will follow his ruin. Once a man is caught in this sin it follows him the rest of his life either by his own guilty conscience, his losses, and by other people. The young man is counselled to confine his enjoyments to their lawful and proper bounds. Because unfaithfulness, adultery and fornication are common today doesn't mean that God has changed His mind or His law about sexual sins. There is great warning throughout the scripture about the consequences of this illegitimate practice. Jesus said in Matthew 5:28 regarding adultery *"But I say to you that whoever looks at a woman to lust for her has already committed adultery with her in his heart."* We need to pray constantly that God will keep our hearts and minds pure. The fashions of today can be a source of enticement which are common even among women who claim the name of Christ. We are admonished in the New Testament to dress in modesty. The man who finds enjoyment within proper bounds will find pleasure and fulfillment with the wife of his youth. Her love alone should allure him (verses 15-19). God knows all that we need and desire and He has created us to experience happiness so that we can know contentment in its purest form as we follow His Word. The iniquities of the wicked will only destroy them and they shall die through the folly of rejecting instructions.

The lust of uncleanness is not only a war against the soul but also against the body.

Daily Bible Study Questions for Group Discussion

Note: Read notes and Scripture references before answering the questions. Some questions are for those more advanced in Bible Study. Try to answer all questions but don't be discouraged if some seem a little hard. Unless otherwise instructed, use Bible only in answering questions.

FIRST DAY. Read notes on Lesson 26.

1. What purpose did Solomon give for writing the Book of Proverbs?

2. As used in the Book of Proverbs, what is the meaning of "prudence"? What is the meaning of "simple"?

3. What are some of the warnings given in these first chapters?

4. To whom is most of the instruction given in these first chapters?

SECOND DAY: Read Proverbs 6 and 7.

5. From **verses 1 through 15 of Proverbs 6**, what three things are dealt with that contribute to poor financial commitments, poverty or a bad reputation? Give verses.

6. (a) List the seven things that God hates.

(b) Has wickedness changed since the days of Solomon? Explain some root causes.

(c) What is given as a deterrent to the things God hates as stated in **Chapter 6**?

THIRD DAY: Read Proverbs 8.

7. **Reread Proverbs 7:5-27** with **Proverbs 8:1-31** and compare and contrast the description of wisdom with that of the strange woman in **Chapter seven**.

8. Compare **Proverbs 8:22-31** with **John 1:1-14; Colossians 1:15-17**. Whom may this be a dim foreshadowing of?

9. What greater gift is offered in Christ? **Read John 17:2-3** with **Proverbs 8:32-36**.

FOURTH DAY. Read Proverbs 9-10.

10. (a) Find the verses in **Chapter 9** where wisdom and the foolish woman both extend an invitation. In what way are they alike and in what do they differ?

(b) What is the positive argument of Wisdom's invitation? What is the negative?

11. In **Chapter 10**, what are the marks of good character that result in the well-being of man in circumstances, mind and character?

12. **James 3:10** states: *"Out of the same mouth proceed blessing and cursing. My brethren, these things ought not to be so."* What uses of speech in Proverbs 10 are to be commended? Which are to be avoided?

FIFTH DAY AND SIXTH DAYS: Read Proverbs 11.

13. Underline on your worksheet **(verses 1 through 23)** the moral principles that are a possession of one who lives righteously.

14. Underline in **Proverbs 11:1-23** with a different color pen, the results of wickedness.

15. In **Proverbs 11** what two kinds of sin are said to be an abomination to the Lord?

16. In **Proverbs 11:30**, consider the fruit and the tree of life. This should encourage us to reach out to others. What are some ways we can make our lives count in winning others for Christ?

Proverbs 11

11:1 Dishonest scales are an abomination to the LORD, But a just weight is His delight.

2 When pride comes, then comes shame; But with the humble is wisdom.

3 The integrity of the upright will guide them, But the perversity of the unfaithful will destroy them.

4 Riches do not profit in the day of wrath, But righteousness delivers from death.

5 The righteousness of the blameless will direct his way aright, But the wicked will fall by his own wickedness.

6 The righteousness of the upright will deliver them, But the unfaithful will be caught by their lust.

7 When a wicked man dies, his expectation will perish, And the hope of the unjust perishes.

8 The righteous is delivered from trouble, And it comes to the wicked instead.

9 The hypocrite with his mouth destroys his neighbor, But through knowledge the righteous will be delivered.

10 When it goes well with the righteous, the city rejoices; And when the wicked perish, there is jubilation.

11 By the blessing of the upright the city is exalted, But it is overthrown by the mouth of the wicked.

12 He who is devoid of wisdom despises his neighbor, But a man of understanding holds his peace.

13 A talebearer reveals secrets, But he who is of a faithful spirit conceals a matter.

14 Where there is no counsel, the people fall; But in the multitude of counselors there is safety.

15 He who is surety for a stranger will suffer, But one who hates being surety is secure.

16 A gracious woman retains honor, But ruthless men retain riches.

17 The merciful man does good for his own soul, But he who is cruel troubles his own flesh.

18 The wicked man does deceptive work, But he who sows righteousness will have a sure reward.

19 As righteousness leads to life, So he who pursues evil pursues it to his own death.

20 Those who are of a perverse heart are an abomination to the LORD, But the blameless in their ways are His delight.

21 Though they join forces, the wicked will not go unpunished; But the posterity of the righteous will be delivered.

22 As a ring of gold in a swine's snout, So is a lovely woman who lacks discretion.

23 The desire of the righteous is only good, But the expectation of the wicked is wrath.

24 There is one who scatters, yet increases more; And there is one who withholds more than is right, But it leads to poverty.

25 The generous soul will be made rich, And he who waters will also be watered himself.

26 The people will curse him who withholds grain, But blessing will be on the head of him who sells it.

27 He who earnestly seeks good finds favor, But trouble will come to him who seeks evil.

28 He who trusts in his riches will fall, But the righteous will flourish like foliage.

29 He who troubles his own house will inherit the wind, And the fool will be servant to the wise of heart.

30 The fruit of the righteous is a tree of life, And he who wins souls is wise.

31 If the righteous will be recompensed on the earth, How much more the ungodly and the sinner.

Notes

Proverbs 6 - 11

I. Proverbs 6

Presented in the first five verses of this Proverb is a warning against foolish financial commitment in becoming surety for the debts of others. Today, this would be termed becoming another's security or to undersign his note or bond. "Striking hands" together was one Hebrew method of publicly assuming financial responsibility. Solomon's advice is very clear regarding the practice of becoming security for another's debts. Proverbs 11:15 also says, *"He who is surety for a stranger will suffer, but one who hates being surety is secure."* Also 17:18, *"A man devoid of understanding shakes hands in a pledge, and becomes surety for his friend"* (Read 20:16; 27:13; 22:26-27).

Verses 6-11 speak of those who love ease and are habitually lazy. Reference to the ant implies this conclusion. Since these insects obey the imperfect instinct and impulse which God has given, how much more should man respond to the dictates of the better instructed mind. We find many other lessons of industry in "the way" of the ant. What Solomon had seen with a clear and accurate eye, and what he wrote has been confirmed by modern science. Verses 10 and 11 express the reply of the sluggard (or lazy one). He is satisfied with the self-indulgence of sleep, caring little for the consequences of folding the hands that should be actively used. Poverty and want follow since bread is gotten only by labor. Luther says the sluggard sins against the very nature which God has given him. *"Go to the ant, you sluggard! Consider her ways and be wise,"* (Proverbs 6:6). She provides for her wants and lays in store for future needs. Children must be taught responsibility. Unless parents teach them early they develop an irresponsible attitude in getting all they can for nothing which results in laziness toward home, school and service to the Lord. A "let someone else do it" attitude can only mean trouble in both youth and adulthood. Some people repeat the words from

Phillipians 4:19, *"And my God shall supply all your need according to His riches in glory by Christ Jesus."* but this is certainly no license for laziness. God has designed that man should diligently work and provide for his family. God also knows of our inabilities and will provide that which we lack. Responsibilities and gifts differ with people. Do well with that which you are capable of doing. God will bless you for it.

Verses 12 to 15 are interesting in regard to the present day use of sign language that is associated with evil. The evil heart has always been the same in its nature and manifestations of signs for words. The wink, the shrug and the fingers are used as a method of insidious meanings (Verse 13).

A summary of evils in the heart and life are given in verses 16-19. There are seven things which God hates: **Pride**, because it is at the root of much sin, **lying** or fraudulence, **hands that shed innocent blood**, **murder, malicious scheming, false charges** or misrepresentation with malicious intent to damage another's character or reputation, and the **sowing of discord** among others. Causing dissent between relatives and neighbors has serious consequences. Dissention is caused when someone uses gossip and wicked means to alienate love for one another. To provoke wrong attitudes one against another brings grief and is the beginning of creating more serious problems. The sin of sowing discord is abhorred by the God of love and peace. Families and neighborhoods can be riddled by it. God himself, by His Word and Holy Spirit, guides, preserves and communes with the obedient heart. A father's commandment and a mother's law are assumed to be identical in their teaching and effects with the law of God. **Christ's Word is sanctifying**. If you love and revere it, it will make a difference in your conduct. The lamp and light will reveal what needs to be changed in character and motive. Then, better than a lamp, it will show the excellence of holiness and help you to grow toward a godly life. **Christ's Word is sustaining**. Daily work needs daily bread and it is in the Bible that the bread of life is stored.

Sensual acts are an abomination both to man and to God. No sin results in greater absurdity and a more fatal lack of discretion, or in a more devastating ruin, than that of sexual sin. A man's good name perishes; no tears can wipe away his reproach. An adulterous man loses credibility with those of either sex and often loses both family and a place of responsibility in the work place. It is a reputation that remains. He is considered morally irresponsible and therefore is not one in which people will place a trust for reliability. Today it also endangers a man's life because of jealously which is the rage of a man.

Many reading these notes could have a sense of discouragement because of the sin of a past life. We learn from God's word about the things He hates. But ever keep in mind the forgiving power and love of Christ. All burden of sin and sins are lifted as we come to the Cross of Christ for forgiveness. Your sin and mine were nailed to the cross and as we come to Him, sins are washed away. How precious this truth is. People who psychologically suffer from guilt are those who have never been to the cross for forgiveness. When one accepts His forgiveness Satan's work is defeated and there is victory in Christ. You become a new creature in Christ Jesus. Never permit Satan to place a guilt trip on you for past sins. We all have a past but for the grace, love, and mercy of God none of us could ever know freedom from guilt.

II. Proverbs 7

In chapters 2, 5, and 6 the great dangers to which the sin of adultery exposes one have been strongly dealt with. Its purpose is to put the virtuous one on their guard, and to make them know the awful abhorrence of the ways of sin. The author sketches a life scene in which are traced:

1. The young man void of understanding, wandering in the dark night (verses 8, 9).

2. A harlot and her vile seductions (verses 10-20).

3. The sudden and fearful ruin in which the harlot involves her victims (verses 21-23).

4. Closing with renewed exhortations against being enticed by one who has ruined her thousands and whose *"house is the way to hell, going down to the chambers of death"* (verses 24-27).

The following is a quote from H. Clay Turmbull, D.D.

"God's Word has its silences, merciful and beneficent; but Satan's word has its silences too, not merciful, and not beneficent. Satan's word tells of flowery paths of alluring pleasures, of seductive companionships, of jovial nights and days; but Satan's word is silent concerning the hidden precipices, the gnawing remorse, the degrading bondage, the deathless despair that lie in wait for the footsteps of those who walk in evil paths. Flashing lights, costly paintings, merry music, send out their welcome to the passer from halls of fair-seeming which are wholly devoted to the service of evil; but no voice from within, no legend on the wall tells of the ruined lives, the scattered households, the broken hearts, whose history found its first tragic meaning beneath these lights."

III. Proverbs 8

Wisdom herself is introduced in this chapter with her own majesty and glory. Her work is seen in the wonders of the universe and in the order of human life. She is co-eternal with God as one with Him, working out His will and is manifested in all His works. In John's Gospel we have the words *"In the beginning was the Word, and the Word was with God, and the Word was God. He was in the beginning with God. All things were made through Him, and without Him nothing was made that was made"* (John 1:1-3). *"He was in the world, and the world was made through Him, and the world did not know Him"* (John 1:10). Christ, who is made unto us sanctification and redemption, is also made unto us wisdom. The eternal Word reveals Himself (verse 31) as One whose *"delights are with the children of men."*

IV. Proverbs 9

This chapter is the closing part of a discourse that began in chapter 6:20 and ends in 9:16. The chapter begins with the declaration that Wisdom has provided herself a house or temple, where preparation is made for the feast to which she invites her chosen guests (verses 1, 2). She sends forth her maidens to summon these guests, yet not every one is invited, only the simple, who lack understanding (verses 3, 4). It would not be appropriate for the scorner and the vile transgressor to be included in the instruction of Wisdom for they would not receive them or profit by them. The guests are invited to a meal not of physical luxuries, but of that which is much better, of exhortation to walk in the way of life (verses 5, 6). Scorners refuse reproof; and it only brings contempt on the reprover (verses 7, 8). This is not true with the wise (verse 9). Wisdom is the fear of God, which has the promise of long life. The word "holy" in verse 10, the knowledge of the holy, refers to God in the special sense of knowing God as the Holy One.

Kitto has an interesting commentary about mingled wine. He says, "in Isaiah 1:22 'wine mixed with water' is expressly mentioned; and this is what we believe to be intended in the present case, as well as in most if not all others in which the term occurs. This impression is confirmed to our mind by the distinct knowledge we possess that the ancients were greatly in the habit of mixing water with their wine, and that pure wine was seldom taken, except in feasts of drunkenness, when it might even be mixed with stronger ingredients. But under all ordinary circumstances the wine was mixed with water, so as to form a table drink, refreshing, but slightly exciting, unless taken in very large quantities. The quantity of water was usually proportioned to the strength of the wine. Sometimes three parts water added to one of wine, and at other times five parts water to one of wine." This also is believed to have been a water purifier.

The book of Proverbs sets before us wisdom or folly. The early chapters show us a picture of a lad, standing at the beginning of his life, and about him are a variety of voices and enticements, some drawing him one way and some another. The picture is youth as it comes to all of us. Temptations and enticements lurk from every side. Parental advice and counselling give words of wisdom. To young men the voices become conflicting. Life becomes reduced to two alternatives, wisdom or folly. **Wisdom** sets in the highest places of the city and cries *"Whoever is simple, let him turn*

in here!" **Folly** sits in the highest places of the city, and cries with the same invitation *"Whoever is simple, let him turn in here!"* They are all either the call of the wisdom of God, or they are the call of folly and sin.

Verse 12 says *"If you are wise, you are wise for yourself, and if you scoff, you will bear it alone."* This teaches that one personally must choose direction. Many try to blame a downfall on another because they don't want to accept responsibility for their choices. We can be tempted and enticed, but our conduct is still our choice. To be tempted is not a sin, but to yield to temptation and enticement is sin. If young people could just realize how important the right turns are, because a wrong turn potentially will follow them through life. In trying to correct one devastating wrong turn, it often begins a chain reaction of many. Every young person should read a chapter in Proverbs each day till consequences of choices are ingrained into their hearts and minds.

In several points description is given in verses 13 to 18, as the foolish woman stands in contrast over against Wisdom as she appears in this chapter. She, too, has a house of her own at the door of which she sits. Her seat is *"in the high places of the city."* These are the same words which are said of Wisdom, (verses 3). Like Wisdom, she invites the simple to turn in hither, and he that wanteth understanding (verse 16); but her arguments are peculiarly her own. *"Stolen water is sweet, and bread eaten in secret is pleasant."* Her appeal turns to the pleasures of sinning. Pleasures of sin are attractive because they are forbidden. The veil is drawn away and behind the scene is the world of the dead. Losing their true life, they are already in the depths of hell. No words can add anything to the awfulness of the warning. The long introduction closes and the collection of separate proverbs begins. Wisdom and folly have each spoken. The issues of each have been painted in life. The learner is left to choice.

V. Proverbs 10

This chapter in the Book of Proverbs begins a distinct division of the book. Its special feature is that each proverb is complete in itself having no apparent connection with what precedes or follows. Usually each proverb is made up of two propositions, one over against the other.

Wisdom and folly in **verse one** are not only in the intellectual sense, but in a moral sense; **wisdom** is a right state of heart and course of life, controlled by the fear of God; **folly**, a wicked heart and life that casts off all fear of God and regard for man.

Treasures of wickedness in verse two are those gotten by oppression, fraud, theft and robbery. Such treasures do not profit and can only result in condemnation by our conscience and judicial courts. Riches with godliness and good conscience are the blessings of God and a benefit to ourselves and others.

Verse 4 — *"He who has a slack hand becomes poor, but the hand of the diligent makes rich."* This applies to both the business life as well as the spiritual. Diligence is necessary in laying up of treasure whether here on earth or in heaven.

Verse 7 — "Memory" and "name" are equivalent terms, both referring to what is thought, said, or felt of men after they are dead.

Verse 9 — *"He who walks with integrity walks securely, but he who perverts his ways will become known."* He knows what guide he follows and what ground he stands on.

Verses 11-21 — There is another subject dealt with in the book; the regulation of the tongue and the power of speech whether for good or evil. The blessing in well chosen words is beautifully represented by a well of life, which brought forth its refreshing waters. The mouth is that through which wisdom or its opposite passes.

Verses 27-30 — These truths are confirmed by the nature of things and the positive appointments of Providence. Men destroy themselves and shorten their lives by many kinds of wickedness. Whole countries are devastated by wars. By domestic quarrels and violence toward others, people bring each other to untimely deaths. By capital crimes they cause themselves to be cut off by the hand of justice. By luxury and intemperance they destroy their bodies. By envy and malice they consume themselves in the midst of their iniquity. In like manner according to the same tendency, by peace and charity men are preserved from destruction; by temperance their bodies are maintained in health; by a good conscience and peace of mind, new life is added to their spirits.

VI. Proverbs 11

This Proverb teaches that the eye of God is upon all transactions, and His heart is in them as well. He disapproves and abhors fraud in trade. He loves the honest dealer. The principle applies to fraud in quality as well as quantity. Our God is a God of justice. The false balance, which is an abomination to the Lord, is all about us. Fraudulent schemes and deceitful practices begin in the heart. An unfair dealer has defrauded himself before he has defrauded another. Honesty is the best policy for personal peace and God's blessing (verse 1).

Pride comes, and then follows shame and disgrace. Opposed to pride there is wisdom. There is no wisdom in pride. It is a sin for which God often brings men down, for He resists the proud (verse 2).

Matthew Henry says, "The integrity of an honest man will itself be his guide in the way of duty and way of safety. His principles are fixed, his rule is certain and therefore, his way is plain; his sincerity keeps him steady, and he needs not change every time the wind turns, having no other end to drive at than to keep a good conscience" (verse 3).

The day of death will be a day of wrath; it is a messenger of God's wrath; therefore, when Moses had meditated on man's mortality, he takes occasion to admire the power of God's anger (Psalm 90:11). It is a debt owing to God's justice. After death the judgment, and that is a day of wrath. Riches will be of no value in that day; they will neither supply excesses nor ease the pain, much less take out the sting; what profit will this world's birthrights be of then? (verse 4).

It is not in man's nature to limit his expectations and hopes at the boundary line of death. He must and will expect to live on beyond that line and will hope for good there; but the wicked man's hope as to that future life will perish. In this life everything for the future is at stake. Death is real; the grave is real, hell is real and the judgment is real. These cannot be changed by the imagination and so consideration for the future must be given serious consideration in the time God gives us now (verse 7).

How easy it is to look at others' errors with a high powered microscope and our own through the wrong end of a telescope and neither are in proper perspective (verse 9).

If we could part with the disposition of compulsive talking and being a peddler of tales, we will have parted with that which, more than anything else, confuses and perplexes and embitters life. It is also true that tongues that gossip would be silent if ears were not open to listen (verse 13).

"Deceitful wages" or work is contrasted in verse 18 with "a sure reward." The wicked will not enjoy the reward they work for. It will prove a delusion. The man who sows righteousness will reap a sure reward. These results follow from the laws of society; and they are sure in the end because God blesses the righteous.

Sowing righteousness is never lost labor. Every act done by God's grace is living and fruitful. It may seem to go out of sight, like seed beneath the ground, but it will rise again. Sow in faith, and you will reap in joy (verse 19).

"Though they join forces, the wicked will not go unpunished;"(verse 21). There is a strange and subtle fascination about a crowd that tends to blind the mind to the sense of sin and danger. It is easier to drift with the crowd than to go against the tide. Seeing that you are one in a great company of others gives you confidence in the direction you are going. If someone suggests you are going the wrong direction the response would be "How could I, I am not alone. Here are rich and poor, learned and ignorant. Much of the best in culture and education and the youth are going the same direction. It certainly cannot be true that this great, busy and joyous crowd is going in the wrong direction". Sin loses its ugly look when it is committed by a majority. Individual responsibility becomes lost in the crowd.

Personal beauty is not a thing to be despised. It is a work of God, and none of His works are done in vain. Beauty is a talent and has a power. If your heart desires the things of God and your objectives are true, personal beauty will double that which you have to give. The important consideration is, 'how may I best use what God has blessed me with to be an instrument to the praise of His glory?' Remember that beauty is more than bodily features; character is beauty. The most ugly, unattractive person can have beauty of character that far surpasses physical beauty (verse 22).

"Scattering" for the good of others does not bring one to poverty. Men may give liberally, and through God's blessing upon them their wealth may increase. On the other hand one who withholds more than is just and right does it to his greater poverty. It cannot be wise to ignore the providence of God. His will is to honor those who honor Him. The law of sowing and reaping is alike in every field. Gain is by scattering rather than by hoarding. He who lives for self will in the end have only self to live for. He who lives for others will sooner or later have others living for him. Love begets love. He who uses his money has more money - more of the best results of money and more of its true enjoyment than one who holds his money. It is not what we have, but what we do with that which we have. That is the real measure of our wealth, our material, our mental and our heart wealth. The right use of His gifts increases them in our hands.

The world has the wrong concept in its pursuit of happiness. They think it consists in having and getting and being served by others. Jesus said that he who would be great should be a servant. The liberal man will always be rich, for his estate is God's providence. God's wisdom and His power are his defense, God's love and favor, his reward, and God's Word, his security. He "that withholds" from the hungry who need bread, hoarding and holding for the sake of a higher price, taking advantage of the necessities of those in need of bread, God will hold those responsible who withhold for personal gain that which is needed to feed the hungry. God's blessing will be upon those who sell promptly in time of need at fair and not at famine prices (verses 24-25-26).

"The fruit of the righteous is a tree of life" because it is a blessed influence toward the winning of souls from sin and a ruined life. *"He who wins souls is wise."* It is the Holy Spirit who draws people to Christ, yet the Spirit works through believers to win unbelievers. "Work upon marble and it will perish, work upon brass and time will change or destroy it, temples will crumble into dust. Work with people and impress on them right principles with the just fear of God. By so doing we engrave upon that which time cannot destroy. In this sense we may all be artists and with a loving heart may produce a masterpiece" (Daniel Webster). There will be those who will never be saved unless we do our part to win them for Christ (verse 30).

Daily Bible Study Questions for Group Discussion

Note: Read notes and Scripture references before answering the questions. Some questions are for those more advanced in Bible Study. Try to answer all questions but don't be discouraged if some seem a little hard. Unless otherwise instructed, use Bible only in answering questions.

FIRST DAY: Read notes on Lesson #27.

1. Give something you learned from your notes about:
   a. Finances

   b. Laziness

   c. Tongue

   d. Beauty

2. What thoughts do you have about the necessity of using Proverbs in teaching young people?

3. What was most meaningful to you either from the notes or lecture?

4. From the notes or scripture text, what is there to learn about choices and responsibilities?

SECOND DAY: Read Proverbs 12 - 13.

5. What does **Proverbs 12** have to say about a woman in relation to her husband?

6. What verses in **Proverbs 12** have to do with agriculture and what two aspects does it mention?

7. What is the sum and substance of **Chapter 12 given in verse 28**.

8. In **Proverbs 13**, two verses give instruction regarding the son. One is the response of a son; the other, an admonishment to a parent. Give the verses and briefly state what responsibility parents have with their children.

THIRD DAY: Read chapters 14-15.

9. In **chapter 14** underline on your text worksheet the verses that have to do with foolishness, fools, and folly.

10. Underline with a different color pen what should be the manner of life for the wise.

11. What **one verse in Proverbs 14** is special to you?

12. (a) In **chapter 15** underline all the verses that have to do with right speech; lips, tongue, prayer, answer, word.

    (b) Underline five things that are sound philosophy for healthy satisfaction.
         (verses 13-17)

FOURTH DAY: Read chapter 16.

13. What two things are given as an abomination in this chapter?

14. What, in **chapter 16**, is said about man's proper attitude toward the Lord?

15. *"How much better is it to get wisdom than gold?"* What are some of the values of both wisdom and gold? Why is wisdom better?

16. What are some characteristics of ungodly and evil men?

FIFTH AND SIXTH DAYS: Read chapter 17.

17. What sins are condemned in **Chapter 17**? Underline them on your text worksheet.

18. In what verse does God show sensitivity to the poor?

19. What is an abomination to God in this chapter?

20. Strife is sometimes compared to fire and sometimes to water. Once loose, they are unmerciful. What verse in **Chapter 17** has to do with strife, water let loose and contention?

Proverbs 14

14:1 The wise woman builds her house, But the foolish pulls it down with her hands.

2 He who walks in his uprightness fears the LORD, But he who is perverse in his ways despises Him.

3 In the mouth of a fool is a rod of pride, But the lips of the wise will preserve them.

4 Where no oxen are, the trough is clean; But much increase comes by the strength of an ox.

5 A faithful witness does not lie, But a false witness will utter lies.

6 A scoffer seeks wisdom and does not find it, But knowledge is easy to him who understands.

7 Go from the presence of a foolish man, When you do not perceive in him the lips of knowledge.

8 The wisdom of the prudent is to understand his way, But the folly of fools is deceit.

9 Fools mock at sin, But among the upright there is favor.

10 The heart knows its own bitterness, And a stranger does not share its joy.

11 The house of the wicked will be overthrown, But the tent of the upright will flourish.

12 There is a way that seems right to a man, But its end is the way of death.

13 Even in laughter the heart may sorrow, And the end of mirth may be grief.

14 The backslider in heart will be filled with his own ways, But a good man will be satisfied from above.

15 The simple believes every word, But the prudent considers well his steps.

16 A wise man fears and departs from evil, But a fool rages and is self-confident.

17 A quick-tempered man acts foolishly, And a man of wicked intentions is hated.

18 The simple inherit folly, But the prudent are crowned with knowledge.

19 The evil will bow before the good, And the wicked at the gates of the righteous.

20 The poor man is hated even by his own neighbor, But the rich has many friends.

21 He who despises his neighbor sins; But he who has mercy on the poor, happy is he.

22 Do they not go astray who devise evil? But mercy and truth belong to those who devise good.

23 In all labor there is profit, But idle chatter leads only to poverty.

24 The crown of the wise is their riches, But the foolishness of fools is folly.

25 A true witness delivers souls, But a deceitful witness speaks lies.

26 In the fear of the LORD there is strong confidence, And His children will have a place of refuge.

27 The fear of the LORD is a fountain of life, To turn one away from the snares of death.

28 In a multitude of people is a king's honor, But in the lack of people is the downfall of a prince.

29 He who is slow to wrath has great understanding, But he who is impulsive exalts folly.

30 A sound heart is life to the body, But envy is rottenness to the bones.

31 He who oppresses the poor reproaches his Maker, But he who honors Him has mercy on the needy.

32 The wicked is banished in his wickedness, But the righteous has a refuge in his death.

33 Wisdom rests in the heart of him who has understanding, But what is in the heart of fools is made known.

34 Righteousness exalts a nation, But sin is a reproach to any people.

35 The king's favor is toward a wise servant, But his wrath is against him who causes shame.

Proverbs 15

15:1 A soft answer turns away wrath, But a harsh word stirs up anger.

2 The tongue of the wise uses knowledge rightly, But the mouth of fools pours forth foolishness.

3 The eyes of the LORD are in every place, Keeping watch on the evil and the good.

4 A wholesome tongue is a tree of life, But perverseness in it breaks the spirit.

5 A fool despises his father's instruction, But he who receives correction is prudent.

6 In the house of the righteous there is much treasure, But in the revenue of the wicked is trouble.

7 The lips of the wise disperse knowledge, But the heart of the fool does not do so.

8 The sacrifice of the wicked is an abomination to the LORD, But the prayer of the upright is His delight.

9 The way of the wicked is an abomination to the LORD, But He loves him who follows righteousness.

10 Harsh discipline is for him who forsakes the way, And he who hates correction will die.

11 Hell and Destruction are before the LORD; So how much more the hearts of the sons of men.

12 A scoffer does not love one who corrects him, Nor will he go to the wise.

13 A merry heart makes a cheerful countenance, But by sorrow of the heart the spirit is broken.

14 The heart of him who has understanding seeks knowledge, But the mouth of fools feeds on foolishness.

15 All the days of the afflicted are evil, But he who is of a merry heart has a continual feast.

16 Better is a little with the fear of the LORD, Than great treasure with trouble.

17 Better is a dinner of herbs where love is, Than a fatted calf with hatred.

18 A wrathful man stirs up strife, But he who is slow to anger allays contention.

19 The way of the lazy man is like a hedge of thorns, But the way of the upright is a highway.

20 A wise son makes a father glad, But a foolish man despises his mother.

21 Folly is joy to him who is destitute of discernment, But a man of understanding walks uprightly.

22 Without counsel, plans go awry, But in the multitude of counselors they are established.

23 A man has joy by the answer of his mouth, And a word spoken in due season, how good it is!

24 The way of life winds upward for the wise, That he may turn away from hell below.

25 The LORD will destroy the house of the proud, But He will establish the boundary of the widow.

26 The thoughts of the wicked are an abomination to the LORD, But the words of the pure are pleasant.

27 He who is greedy for gain troubles his own house, But he who hates bribes will live.

28 The heart of the righteous studies how to answer, But the mouth of the wicked pours forth evil.

29 The LORD is far from the wicked, But He hears the prayer of the righteous.

30 The light of the eyes rejoices the heart, And a good report makes the bones healthy.

31 The ear that hears the rebukes of life Will abide among the wise.

32 He who disdains instruction despises his own soul, But he who heeds rebuke gets understanding.

33 The fear of the LORD is the instruction of wisdom, And before honor is humility.

Proverbs 17

17:1 Better is a dry morsel with quietness, Than a house full of feasting with strife.

2 A wise servant will rule over a son who causes shame, And will share an inheritance among the brothers.

3 The refining pot is for silver and the furnace for gold, But the LORD tests the hearts.

4 An evildoer gives heed to false lips; A liar listens eagerly to a spiteful tongue.

5 He who mocks the poor reproaches his Maker; He who is glad at calamity will not go unpunished.

6 Children's children are the crown of old men, And the glory of children is their father.

7 Excellent speech is not becoming to a fool, Much less lying lips to a prince.

8 A present is a precious stone in the eyes of its possessor; Wherever he turns, he prospers.

9 He who covers a transgression seeks love, But he who repeats a matter separates friends.

10 Rebuke is more effective for a wise man Than a hundred blows on a fool.

11 An evil man seeks only rebellion; Therefore a cruel messenger will be sent against him.

12 Let a man meet a bear robbed of her cubs, Rather than a fool in his folly.

13 Whoever rewards evil for good, Evil will not depart from his house.

14 The beginning of strife is like releasing water; Therefore stop contention before a quarrel starts.

15 He who justifies the wicked, and he who condemns the just, Both of them alike are an abomination to the LORD.

16 Why is there in the hand of a fool the purchase price of wisdom, Since he has no heart for it?

17 A friend loves at all times, And a brother is born for adversity.

18 A man devoid of understanding shakes hands in a pledge, And becomes surety for his friend.

19 He who loves transgression loves strife, And he who exalts his gate seeks destruction.

20 He who has a deceitful heart finds no good, And he who has a perverse tongue falls into evil.

21 He who begets a scoffer does so to his sorrow, And the father of a fool has no joy.

22 A merry heart does good, like medicine, But a broken spirit dries the bones.

23 A wicked man accepts a bribe behind the back To pervert the ways of justice.

24 Wisdom is in the sight of him who has understanding, But the eyes of a fool are on the ends of the earth.

25 A foolish son is a grief to his father, And bitterness to her who bore him.

26 Also, to punish the righteous is not good, Nor to strike princes for their uprightness.

27 He who has knowledge spares his words, And a man of understanding is of a calm spirit.

28 Even a fool is counted wise when he holds his peace; When he shuts his lips, he is considered perceptive.

Notes

Proverbs 12-17

I. Proverbs 12

Solomon began this proverb by comparing the wise and the foolish; the righteous and the wicked. The continuing theme is that of strength with the underlying simile of a tree with strong roots and the righteous man.

Well rooted, standing strong, the righteous man is unmovable. The wicked never get a firm footing or rooting and are blown down, torn up by the roots and left to deteriorate with the changing climatic atmosphere.

"A virtuous woman" is a crown to her husband. The *"prudent wife"* is considered one of God's best gifts, *"building her house"* or making a house a "home" with her love and care. In her excellence she is the crown and glory of a man's life. A picture of ideal happiness is made perfect with the brightness of this true union whose relationship is built on the only true foundation, love of God and love for each other. Her influence on her children is as great, if not greater than that of a father. They owe what they have of goodness to her loving influence. What greater place of importance can a woman have than to be a prudent wife to her husband and a loving mother to her children?

There is the fatal, inevitable fact in verse 7 that says the wicked are overthrown and there is nothing left for them till they stand before the righteous judge for eternal sentencing. *"The house of the righteous will stand."*

In verse 14 the fruit of the mouth is what the mouth speaks. The supposition is that a righteous man will speak in harmony with his character. What he does, as well as what he says, will be beneficial to others as well as to himself. Words and action on the part of man, his speech and conduct, are representative of what a person is in character.

The meaning of the proverb in verse 15 is that the way of the fool is so right in his own eyes that he will not listen to counsel. Listening to good counsel is characteristic of the wise but not of the fool.

"The tongue of the wise promotes health." It gives healing. Their words lovingly heal the wounds which the slanderer inflicts. There is balm in healing words. It is important to use our gift of speech to give comfort, joy, cheer and hope to those around us. Use it to encourage the weary and disheartened. Use it also in love to warn those who are treading in paths of danger.

"The truthful lip shall be established forever, but a lying tongue is but for a moment." The love of truth gives stability to character. You may get by in the world without it but never to the satisfaction of your own heart or the smile and approval of God (verse 19).

"Lying lips are an abomination to the Lord, but those who deal truthfully are His delight." Falsehood is a contradiction to God and a deliberate intent to deceive. The dictionary definition of lying is to make an untrue statement with intent to deceive; to create a false or misleading impression or a falseness or unreliability in statement or dealings (verse 22). The word "heaviness" in verse 25 means anxiety or fear which gives a sense of heaviness or being depressed, *"But a good word makes it glad."* Speaking a kind word, which takes but a moment, can make a heavy heart glad.

Verse 28 is the sum and substance of this chapter and a proper conclusion to all that has been taught.

The only sure way to happiness, to life, is to follow the Lord in the way of righteousness.

II. Proverbs 13

This proverb continues the contrast of the righteous and the wicked showing mostly the advantage of the righteous. *"He who guards his mouth preserves his life, but he who opens wide his lips shall have destruction."* (verse 3). One must have a command of himself when he is provoked so as not to offend with his tongue or in word. Allowing anger to get the better of us creates an atmosphere of hollowness, unstableness and unfaithfulness. Unfaithfulness to ourselves and to others. Weeds of ill feeling begin to sprout and are soon the master over the fruit in our lives. It is a fact that a large portion of the Bible deals with sins of the tongue. If we took all the verses in the Book of Proverbs which have reference to foolish talk or too much talk and bad talk, there would be many. The warnings against these sins are deeply serious because they affect every part of our life. Again we need to pray each day, Psalm 19:14: *"Let the **words of my mouth** and the meditation of my heart be acceptable in Your sight, O Lord, my strength and my Redeemer."*

Verse 4 reminds us of the characteristics of a lazy person. A person who is indolent or lazy has no appreciation of the rights of others. They live with little or no effort on the fruits of the labors of those around them. It becomes a habit of mind to think of things, pleasures and persons as belonging to themselves. This is true in spiritual things. If the heart of a spiritually lazy person should be filled according to his desires, he would have little or nothing. Personal Bible Study for many takes too much effort. Serving in some capacity in the church takes too much effort, so they become inactive and are satisfied to eat and drink as others prepare and serve. To some it is too much effort to get ready and attend the place of worship that they might eat and drink at the refreshing fountain of what God has for them (verse 4).

"Righteousness guards him whose way is blameless, but wickedness overthrows the sinner" (verse 6). If a man will serve his sin, one thing is sure: his sin will find him out, his path will be hard and there will be no peace. The little things of today become the avalanche of tomorrow.

"Wealth gained by dishonesty will be diminished, but he who gathers by labor will increase" (verse 11). The word vanity could be "slight effort, or no effort." Everything valuable which man possesses is the product of some diligent hand of which the laborer is the benefactor. That which we receive through honest work will increase. It will be an inheritance (verse 11). In verse 18 "reproof" has the broad meaning of instruction and good counsel, designed to make one better. To follow such counsel will bring one to honor. Character and life will be improved, faults corrected which will attract esteem and honor to the individual. To reject instruction will end in shame and poverty.

"He who walks with wise men will be wise, but the companion of fools will be destroyed." (verse 20). This proverb gives insight into the power of the social law. The influence of associates — good for good, evil for evil and its consequences. The Bible gives guidance regarding the influence of daily companions upon our life and character. There is an assumption that we become what our companions are. Our companions either have a good influence on us or bad. A good friend is a choice book through whom we can learn precious treasures and our life can be enriched (verse 20).

"He who spares his rod hates his son, but he who loves him disciplines him promptly" (verse 24). "Rod" in this verse means correction. It is a symbol of that authority which God has committed to fathers and mothers for training their children. The parent is to exercise that authority kindly, yet firmly, wisely and prayerfully. If children are not taught to obey parents at home they will not grow up to be a law-abiding citizen and loyal subjects of the kingdom of God. Children do not naturally tend to be obedient and under authority. This must be taught by the parents with love and care. This principle is imperative for home, school, church and nation. It is unfair to a child not to teach him that there is authority at home and in the community that must be obeyed. We must live within bounds whether or not we prefer it. Our prisons and institutions are overcrowded with those who never learned to respect parents, then God, then the laws in our country. It is a commandment from the Lord that children obey their parents. Parents in turn are to instruct, nurture, and love their children. Discipline

in the home will mean discipline in our schools and country. Teachers in schools were never delegated to teach discipline. Parents should give disciplined children to the school so the teachers can teach their subject without spending most classroom time handling discipline problems. We expect the teachers to do what God has delegated to the parent and also to do their work in teaching reading, writing and arithmetic. Think about it and take seriously your responsibility as parents.

III. Proverbs 14

"The wise woman builds her house, but the foolish pulls it down with her hands" (verse 1). The "woman" (wife) is thought of as a manager of her domestic concerns. Managing them wisely, she increases the comforts of her family. The foolish woman, managing badly, reverses this process and destroys her house.

In verse 6 the scorner is put over against the man of understanding. Having challenged God by their scorn, they spend their time in much learning, yet never coming to the knowledge of the truth for *"A scoffer seeks wisdom and does not find it,"* Getting into any scornful way is fatal. Doubt is reason, scorn is disease. One simply questions, searching after evidence; the other has evidence but it turns to mockery. Even if truth were found, it could not remain in the scorner. A scorner never welcomes truth. No man will seek after truth who does not have a reverence for it.

"Fools mock at sin, but among the upright there is favor." The fool scoffs at the idea of personal sin and guilt. Society is left to the mercy of their perverse and bold humor directed against morals. This is a fearful thing before God. It is because of ignorance that many make a mockery of sin. The wages with which sin bargains with the sinner are life, pleasure, and profit; but its wages with which it pays are death and destruction. Mockery can be made of sin by words and actions. We show it in our actions when we live in such a manner that proves we have no value or regard for it. It is the folly of provoking God to cut us off in the midst of our wickedness. To really know what sin is we must see it in light of redemption. Who can measure the guilt and power of sin from which we could only be redeemed by the sacrifice of the Son of God? (verse 9).

"The heart knows its own bitterness, and a stranger does not share its joy" (verse 10). There is something in every sorrow and in every joy which no one else can share. For the most part we are strangers to the inner life of others, to their thoughts and feelings, their joys and sorrow and they alike are strangers to ours. Only God knows our hearts. When our sympathy for the sufferings of our friends is deepest, we sit with them and are silent. We cannot say what we feel; our tears and our silence seem to tell them more than our speech. Every man bears his own burden, fights his own battle, and walks in a path that no others have trodden. God alone knows what goes on inside. He will come into the stillness and solitude and make the darkness bright with His presence. He alone can understand. He will rejoice with us when we rejoice, and weep with us when we weep. The heart knows its own bitterness: God knows it, too.

"There is a way that seems right to a man, but its end is the way of death."

The way of living may seem right to a man, and yet be wrong and end in death. Men may be deceived by their associates or they may deceive themselves. There is a saying, "It matters not what a man believes, provided he is sincere." This is a fatal mistake. A man often is sincerely wrong in pursuing a fatally wrong course in life. The way of ignorance and carelessness, the way of worldliness and the way of sensuality seem right to those that walk in them. God does not permit us to content ourselves in anything short of truth. He marks a plain path for us to follow; and gives us no reason to believe that anything but truth will save us. Sincerity does not alter truth. God has said that no one shall be saved except through repentance. To think otherwise, even though very sincere in one's opinion, the truth of what God said remains. Christ long ago declared that *"For everyone practicing evil hates the light and does not come to the light, lest his deeds should be exposed"* (John 3:20). Sincerity in error often comes from willful blindness and also from indifference to the will of God. God does not give His law to be trifled with.

"Even in laughter the heart may sorrow, and the end of mirth may be grief" (verse 13). The reaction which follows laughter is often the most painful. It can potentially cover hidden sorrow (verse 13).

"In the fear of the Lord there is strong confidence, and His children will have a place of refuge" (verse 26). Love which destroyed fear heightens a deep reverence for God. *"Perfect love casts out fear,"* (John 4:18) and that, in the Lord, is strong confidence.

"Righteousness exalts a nation, but sin is a reproach to any people" (verse 34).

This proverb speaks of righteousness and sin as having to do with either the government or the general character of a people, and possibly to both. The government generally reflects the average sentiment and character of the people. This is not a matter of strength or weakness but a matter of honor and shame. There are a lot of good and positive things going on in our world today. There are open doors and opportunities presenting themselves as most of us have not seen in our lifetime. Yet, on the other hand, when we see and hear of legalized injustices that are in total opposition to God's Word we wonder if the world is not ripe for God's judgment. The dignity of man is lost for the whims of the unrighteous cries of a segment of society. God will bring judgment for sins of immorality which are the cause of our problems today. The government is spending millions of dollars to combat the evils whose roots are in immorality. Sin is a costly reproach to many people. Why should not the true church (believers in Christ) rise up against it? Christ is the answer, let us work a little harder to proclaim Christ and teach God's Word.

IV. Proverbs 15

"A soft answer turns away wrath, but a harsh word stirs up anger." Gentle words, a forgiving spirit, will do what angry, abusive words and a belligerent attitude never can accomplish. Kind words produce kind actions. It is absolutely necessary for us to remain masters of ourselves in a verbal confrontation. The power of speech and the use we make of it is important. We use it as stewards who are to give account. Verse 4 says, *"A wholesome tongue is a tree of life, but perverseness in it breaks the spirit."*

"In the house of the righteous there is much treasure, but in the revenue of the wicked is trouble" (verse 6). In the house of the righteous there is contentment and love which binds hearts together. God

dwells in the house of the righteous; from above, from within, before our eyes, God in the heart; God in prosperity, God in pain; God as guide of our hearts and minds; God in light and darkness; can there be greater treasure than this? Every heart that God has touched would have to give positive affirmation. *"But in the revenue of the wicked is trouble."* Sin will poison the richest treasure of a household and the most happy marriage.

"The lips of the wise disperse knowledge, but the heart of the fool does not do so" (verse 7). It is not wise to discuss personalities in our general conversation. Talk of things, objects, and thoughts. Do not needlessly report bad things about others. Dwell on the good in individuals. In today's world, the sensational and the down side of life and events are reported to keep people interested!

This is a bad mind-set. When we follow a constant process of deprecating, assigning motives, and cutting up character, it often becomes nothing but lies based on supposition which is a destroyer of other people's character and ends in devastating situations. Only God knows the capabilities of evil in man and it is not our responsibility to detail and report it all. Always be a contributor of building rather than tearing down and destroying others. In conversation keep the atmosphere as pure as possible.

Verse 8 carries with it the meaning that the sacrifice offered by the wicked is abhorred by God for two reasons: (1) It lacks sincere love, the element of true worship and often the motive is to have God's favor upon a life of sin. (2) It desires to buy indulgence. On the other hand, the prayer of the upright, even though he may have no costly sacrifice to give, is God's delight. God delights in a sincere offering from the heart.

"A merry heart makes a cheerful countenance, but by sorrow of the heart the spirit is broken" (verse 13). God made both tears and laughter and had a purpose for both. Tears keep sorrows from becoming despair and madness; and laughter is one of the privileges of reason. Laughter brings relaxation from tension. God gives us the capacity for enjoyment and accepts laughter and cheerfulness as recreation in the real work of life. Christians should be happy, cheerful people. Christ within gives us a

peace and joy that the world cannot give, nor can take away. Verse 15 says *"he who is of a merry heart has a continual feast."* It is like a perpetual feast and an enduring source of pleasure.

"A man has joy by the answer of his mouth, and a word spoken in due season, how good it is!" (verse 23). There is the word of warning: the word of encouragement; the word of sympathy; the word of congratulation; the word of explanation and apology. To be "a son of consolation," to be able to make life a little sweeter and more meaningful for others; good a little easier, evil a little more hated and despised, this would be a privilege to us. "Words" can do much in our Christian life "spoken in due season." Consider the blessing in the words of Isaiah, *"The Lord God has given Me the tongue of the learned, that I should know how to speak a word in season to him who is weary"* (Isa. 50:4). If God has not given to each of us the tongue of the learned, He has given to each, if we will but use it, the tongue of truth, kindness, purity and sympathy.

"The thoughts of the wicked are an abomination to the Lord, but the words of the pure are pleasant" (verse 26). A person's speech is the best manifestation of character. It expresses what is inside of us by air, articulated and made audible by the breath of the mouth. An uncontrolled tongue is a sign of a heart within him being uncontrolled. On the contrary an offenseless tongue is evidence of one who can control his heart and spirit. Learn to speak about others that which edifies.

Verse 28 is a contrast between the "studying" of the wise before he answers and the hasty "babbling" of the foolish. In other words, think before you speak. Hasty words, more often, stir up anger.

"The Lord is far from the wicked, but He hears the prayer of the righteous" (verse 29). The promises made concerning prayer form the main subject of all the promises in the Bible. It has been the resource in seeking truth, in doing that which God has called us, in resisting temptation, in enduring affliction and in preparing to meet death. Living in an attitude of prayer is a beautiful discipline. *"Pray without ceasing"* (I Thessalonians 5:17). Meeting each situation with a dependence on God to help you say

and do the right thing. These prayers are not audible but are silent arrow prayers soliciting God's help for others or for yourself. "God help" is a brief "arrow" prayer. Sometimes that's all we have time to pray but it is a recognition of your only source of help. All prayer that is in faith includes leaving it in God's hands to give or to withhold that for which we have desired in prayer. Leave every situation trustfully with God. A petition may be refused in love, yet in God's wisdom answered in another way, not always obvious to the one who prays.

"The fear of the Lord is the instruction of wisdom, and before honor is humility." (verse 33). Humility is always ready to give place; pride is always disputing about preference. The answer to Augustine to the question, "What is the first thing in religion? Humility. And what is the second? Humility. And what is the third? Humility." Augustine said truly, when speaking of pride, "That which first overcame man is the last thing he overcomes." Humility is the same disposition which the psalmist called a broken heart, and that consciousness of need which Jesus had in mind when He said, *"Blessed are the poor in spirit"* (Matt 5:3). Submissiveness, willing to do what God desires, not being indignant at being overlooked, modesty which is not aware of its own importance, which *"love does not envy; love does not parade itself, is not puffed up; does not behave rudely, does not seek its own, is not provoked, thinks no evil"* (I Corinthians 13:4-5).

V. Proverbs 16

The first seven verses mention the name of the Lord in each verse as Giver, Guide, Ruler or Judge. Preparation of the heart and answer of the tongue are from the Lord. The Lord weighs the spirits. Commit your works to the Lord. The Lord made all for Himself. The proud in heart are an abomination to the Lord. By the fear of the Lord men depart from evil. When man's ways please the Lord, He makes his enemies to be at peace with him. In verse one, the meaning of the proverb covers both the offering of prayer with its answers from the Lord. Verse two says we are blind to our own faults and do not see ourselves as others see us. God is a discerner of the thoughts and intents of the heart. God puts our thoughts and actions in balance. Verse three - commit your burdens to the Lord. He will make your plans firm and successful.

The will of the Lord is done. Commit your works to the Lord and leave them trustfully in His care. He who has the blessing that makes rich, adds no sorrow. Verse four, *"The Lord has made all for Himself, yes, even the wicked for the day of doom."* The meaning of this is that God has so arranged things that punishment will certainly follow one who rejects God and chooses wickedness unless he turns from evil and repents. God has made provision through Christ for the salvation of mankind. However, this is conditional in that man turn to Christ and repent of his sin. If he refuses to repent God has ordained a day of judgment. God brings judgment on the wicked for their voluntary rebellion against His authority, for their antagonism toward all righteousness, goodness and truth. Man is a free moral agent who personally chooses to follow in God's way or reject Him and follow Satan. If man chooses Satan he has chosen God's judgment. People must accept responsibility for their choices. Verse five - see Psalm 11:2. Verse six - the guilt of sin is taken away from us by the mercy and truth of God. Verse seven - a good man will be blessed of God and have peace even with his enemies.

"A man's heart plans his way, but the Lord directs his steps" (verse 9). Man's calculating is often in the dark. We come to the conclusion that we are not our own masters nor the authors of our own destinies, that there is a hand which overrules us. God knows the future and often brings our best laid plans to ruin. This reminds us of our dependance on the great Master of our lives. We are under the hand of our Almighty God. The unseen hand casts the shuttle its own way, and the loom clanks and yields its many colored threads in its own time and fashion. It is true that we can affect the weaving of our own life; we can brighten the colors; we can change the pattern. By our living therefore, we can furnish better material to Him who is the Master weaver.

"The silver-haired head is a crown of glory, if it is found in the way of righteousness" (verse 31). The senior years have beauty the same as youth. The wheel of time cannot be stopped, but the spirit can remain youthful. Living a life dedicated to God and His service can prolong the youthfulness of the spirit. No artist has ever painted an old angel. Fullness of eternal life keeps the aging young. If there is "life"

and "godliness", youth is not a blunder, but a wise purpose and a glowing hope; manhood is a conquest and joy, old age is a rich memory and a glorious prospect.

"He who is slow to anger is better than the mighty, and he who rules his spirit than he who takes a city" (verse 32). Spiritual strength consists of two things: power of will and power of self-restraint. Two things are required for its existence: strong feelings and strong commands over them. Often we mistake strong feelings for strong character. The strength of a man can be measured by the power of the feelings which he subdues, not by the power of those which subdue him. How many Christians are cursed with barrenness and leanness of soul because of a temper which they never learned to control. The Holy Spirit is grieved by a hot, out of control, bad temper. The Holy Spirit is love, tenderness, and gentleness. The angry man cannot pray. Surely God who loves His children and desires their happiness, is not pleased that they should be under the dominion of this evil passion. Victory is available and one needs to pray and believe God that he may be able to overcome and be adorned with a meek and quiet spirit. Don't be discouraged, keep working at it. It takes discipline and that is never conquered in a day. God is gracious and will help you.

VI. Proverbs 17

"The refining pot is for silver and the furnace for gold, but the Lord tests the hearts." Silver and gold are seldom found in the earth without dross: but through *"the refining pot for silver. . .the furnace for gold"* (verse 3). God has trials for the heart of man; whatever fault is in him, no matter how subtle or how carefully covered it may be, God has us in the furnace of trial and correction to burn out the dross and perfect us in such a way that our lives will be more precious than gold. He sits as a refiner and purifier.

"He who covers a transgression seeks love, but he who repeats a matter separates friends" (verse 9). One who does not reveal an offence done to him by his friends, takes a course to maintain friendship and love.

"The beginning of strife is like releasing water; therefore stop contention before a quarrel starts" (verse 14). Where water is damned up, a small break in the dam causes a rush of water, which widens that flow until it runs out of control. So with strife, though seemingly trifling at first, becomes a major problem. Once strife is out of control who can control it?

"A friend loves at all times, and a brother is born for adversity" (verse 17). In adversity as well as in prosperity, a true friend will love. A faithful friend is one to whom we may share our joys, fears, griefs, hopes, counsels, or whatever is upon the heart. A true friend is not born every day. Friends should be those whose companionship is an inspiration, strength and encouragement. A friend is someone in whom you can confide through times of difficulties, sorrow and failures: a friend is someone who knows the best and the worst of us and who loves us in spite of all our faults, who will speak the honest truth to us while the world flatters us to our face but is the opposite behind our back. The bond of friendship will not be broken by trivial matters.

"A merry heart does good, like medicine, but a broken spirit dries the bones" (verse 22). Medicines are either preventive or curative: but prevention is better than cure. A cheerful heart is both preventive and a cure. A broken spirit, burdened by afflictions, and especially a conscience with a sense of guilt and fear, "dries the bones".

"Even a fool is counted wise when he holds his peace; when he shuts his lips, he is considered perceptive." One who is a thinker says little in proportion to his thoughts. He selects language which will convey his ideas in an explicit and distinct manner (verse 28).

Daily Bible Study Questions for Group Discussion

Note: Read notes and Scripture references before answering the questions. Some questions are for those more advanced in Bible Study. Try to answer all questions but don't be discouraged if some seem a little hard. Unless otherwise instructed, use Bible only in answering questions.

FIRST DAY: Read notes on Lesson 28.

1. What subject in this group of Proverbs was most interesting to you?

2. What is the dictionary definition of *lying*?

3. What are some helpful characteristics about the tongue and speech in this lesson?

4. Could you basically agree with the comments on parents, children and authority? (See page 87 of your notes)

SECOND DAY: Read Proverbs 18 -19.

5. Underline on your text worksheet all the verses that have to do with: words, lips, mouth, and tongue in **Chapter 18**.

6. What hidden gem do we find in this chapter that would be an encouragement to both young men and young women?

7. Describe the *friends* mentioned in **Proverbs 19**?

8. What two kinds of wives are mentioned in **Proverbs 19**?

THIRD DAY: Read Proverbs 20-21.

9. What is particularly mentioned in **Proverbs 20** as being an abomination to the Lord?

10. What is said regarding a child in **Chapter 20** that would cause parents to take seriously their responsibility of training a child from early age?

11. In **Chapter 21**, what is more pleasing to God than sacrifice?

12. Complete the following proverbs:

   A. *"Better to dwell in a corner of a housetop,*_____

   _____ *."*

   B. *"Better to dwell in the wilderness,* _____

   _____ *."*

FOURTH DAY: Read chapter 22.

13. What six things are said about the Lord in **Chapter 22**?

14. What **two verses** admonish parents again regarding children? Give the reasons for this advice.

15. What two things are more important than riches and silver and gold that are determined by your choice?

16. From **verses 24-29 in Chapter 22**, make a list of advice given.

FIFTH AND SIXTH DAYS: Read Proverbs 23-24.

17. What warnings are given in the first eight verses concerning food and deceitfulness?

18. What instructive warnings are given a son by his parents?

19. **Read verses 29-35**. Give an answer to each question asked in **verse 29**.

20. What **one verse in Chapter 24** would remind us of the philosophy of the "Golden Rule" in the New Testament? **Read Matthew 7:12.**

Proverbs 18

18:1 A man who isolates himself seeks his own desire; He rages against all wise judgment.

2 A fool has no delight in understanding, But in expressing his own heart.

3 When the wicked comes, contempt comes also; And with dishonor comes reproach.

4 The words of a man's mouth are deep waters; The wellspring of wisdom is a flowing brook.

5 It is not good to show partiality to the wicked, Or to overthrow the righteous in judgment.

6 A fool's lips enter into contention, And his mouth calls for blows.

7 A fool's mouth is his destruction, And his lips are the snare of his soul.

8 The words of a talebearer are like tasty trifles, And they go down into the inmost body.

9 He who is slothful in his work Is a brother to him who is a great destroyer.

10 The name of the LORD is a strong tower; The righteous run to it and are safe.

11 The rich man's wealth is his strong city, And like a high wall in his own esteem.

12 Before destruction the heart of a man is haughty, And before honor is humility.

13 He who answers a matter before he hears it, It is folly and shame to him.

14 The spirit of a man will sustain him in sickness, But who can bear a broken spirit?

15 The heart of the prudent acquires knowledge, And the ear of the wise seeks knowledge.

16 A man's gift makes room for him, And brings him before great men.

17 The first one to plead his cause seems right, Until his neighbor comes and examines him.

18 Casting lots causes contentions to cease, And keeps the mighty apart.

19 A brother offended is harder to win than a strong city, And contentions are like the bars of a castle.

20 A man's stomach shall be satisfied from the fruit of his mouth, From the produce of his lips he shall be filled.

21 Death and life are in the power of the tongue, And those who love it will eat its fruit.

22 He who finds a wife finds a good thing, And obtains favor from the LORD.

23 The poor man uses entreaties, But the rich answers roughly.

24 A man who has friends must himself be friendly, But there is a friend who sticks closer than a brother.

Notes

Proverbs 18 - 24

I. Proverbs 18

"*A man who isolates himself seeks his own desire; he rages against all wise judgment.*" In the first verse of this proverb, we have implied that diversions can give one balance in life. It also gives us some thought about social and unsocial behavior. One who dislikes other people separates himself from others, seeks places to be alone and disapproves any form of diversion or pleasure. Psychologically this is not a healthy situation. Such a person needs to work on his disposition so as to be pleasant and sociable. Very often unsociable people withdraw from the norms of society and find themselves living a very selfish, self-centered life. Diversions are necessary to relieve tensions from the cares, that in routine, can be burdensome and depressing. This will not make one exempt from the God-given responsibilities of family of which husband, wife and children should share in relaxation together. Studies, computers, office work etc., can be very confining and families need to know diversion. A good time for diversion is when, as a family, you can enjoy something together. The pursuit for wisdom is excellent and this we must do, but we must not nullify what wisdom and common sense teach us about relaxation and diversion.

"*It is not good to show partiality to the wicked, or to overthrow the righteous in judgment*" (verse 5). It is not good to respect a wicked person for the purpose of frustrating the righteous in judgment. Such regard for wicked persons is a sin before God, not only because He hates injustice, but especially because this form of injustice frustrates the very provisions God has made for securing justice to those who are both innocent and powerless to assert and maintain it.

Verses 6 and 7 go together, speaking of the results of the "fool's" temper. First there is "contention," then "strokes," then "destruction."

"*The words of a talebearer are like tasty trifles, and they go down into the inmost body*" (verse 8). In other words they make one sick. They are deeper than surface wounds. The malicious gossip of a slanderer is likely to defeat its purpose by its obvious malice. A slander that is simply repeated by one person after another, with its steady increase of scope and explicitness as a matter of gossip, or as a matter of popular information, and often which seems too natural to be a fabrication, gradually gains acceptance that belongs to established truth. It is "they say," that slips so easily from the unwatched, undisciplined tongue, and enters freely into an unguarded ear. There are times and places where slander concerning innocent and unsuspicious persons is passed from one to another unthinkingly, on the basis or the baselessness, of this indefinite origin. If you consent to hear such a charge against another without giving it a challenge, it is, in a sense, giving approval to slander. To pass such gossip to others which has been heard, that person also becomes a slanderer.

"*The spirit of a man will sustain him in sickness, but who can bear a broken spirit?*" (verse 14). Infirmity has to do with pain in the body; a wounded spirit is a mind, sad and cast down.

The first can be endured by firmness and resolution, but a wounded spirit, who can endure it? Another text (verse 19) tells us that a wounded or (violated) spirit "*harder to win than a strong city, and contentions are like the bars of a castle.*" I think of this in the sense of not only a wounded spirit but also wounded love. When one has loved and that love has been rejected or violated, it is almost impossible to establish a trustful spirit of one so seriously wounded. Apart from the mercy and grace of God it is difficult for reconciliation. Examples are in the marriage covenant, between friends in a breach of confidence and violation in business commitments. The marriage covenant is the most violated and serious because generally husband or wife are not the only victims but children are more so. A father or a mother (generally for selfish reasons) violate a marriage contract with little or no concern for the long term or life time effect it has on their children. May God help us to be serious about marriage contracts. Marriage was never intended as an open door that one could walk in and out of. It is a lifetime covenant and commitment before God and man (verses 14 and 19).

"The first one to plead his cause seems right, until his neighbor comes and examines him" (verse 17).

There is a difference between religious controversy and religious discussion. Controversy is contradiction. Discussion is examination. The one is more of an intellectual battle. The other is cooperative study. The purpose of one is victory - the other of truth. The two are distinguishable from each other by the spirit they each manifest. Controversy is angered by opposing truth and tries to pervert it. Discussion gladly recognizes an opposing truth and reconstructs for its reception. Discussion is modest and not self- seeking. Controversy is loud and sometimes unrestrained (verse 17).

"He who finds a wife finds a good thing, and obtains favor from the Lord" (verse 22). A good wife is a blessing which God gives. Marriage is endorsed as a Divine institution and a source of blessing to the husband whose concern it is to find a wife.

"A man who has friends must himself be friendly, but there is a friend who sticks closer than a brother" (verse 24). We all need to have a friend who can keep near us and understand us better, stand by us faithfully and help us. Christ is such a friend. Think of His power - His power to help and protect, in work, in danger and in temptation. He can understand all we are feeling and going through. This best friend will never disappoint us. He is always near. He never fails.

II. Proverbs 19

"Houses and riches are an inheritance from fathers, but a prudent wife is from the Lord" (verse 14).

Prudent here in this verse means wise and intelligent and well-qualified to handle the responsibilities of her position. Houses and lands were inherited by the sons from a father, but a prudent wife comes from the Lord.

"He who has pity on the poor lends to the Lord, and He will pay back what he has given" (verse 17). It is assumed in this text that concern for the poor does not expend itself in emotion, but yields the genuine fruits of substantial help according to our ability and their need. Giving to the poor in the spirit of such true concern virtually lends to the Lord upon His promise to repay in His own due time. What an investment this is! The cup of cold water, given in Christ's name, is emblematic of all those hidden deeds which are nothing in the eyes of men, but are of infinite worth in the eyes of God. The poorest, in their poverty, can share by giving a glass of water. The value of an action does not depend on what we do but the spirit in which it is done. Deeds can be praised by the public, yet be consumed as stubble and as chaff if given in the wrong spirit, The widow's mite, the bit of bread given in love, the word of comfort, the prayer of intercession heard by God alone, will shine as precious metals and jewels in the great day of final judgment. Giving is difficult for a lot of people, yet God blesses those who share with others in need. It is not only money that we need to share, but our time and talent. Visiting the sick, helping the widow, teaching the underprivileged. By teaching, you help people to become self-supporting. We assume dependency on the government but this is not in the plan and purpose of God. People make a difference by giving of themselves. You will be blessed for sharing. Money sometimes is the easiest thing to give for it doesn't necessarily involve you as a person. Careless, **indiscriminate** giving encourages idleness. Carefully inquire for and give relief to people who have experienced unavoidable misfortune. Countries in which little children are dying from starvation and disease need our help if we can get help to them through reliable organizations. God will not suffer His children to beg bread. Those who are able-bodied should be willing to work for their food and shelter if there is nothing more they can do. Laziness is an abomination to the Lord.

"There are many plans in a man's heart, nevertheless the Lord's counsel; that will stand" (verse 21). "A man's heart" is a little world of scheming and business. He may have plans and designs that the business cannot go on without him, but he must know also that God has a plan of His own for every one of us.

III. Proverbs 20

"Wine is a mocker, strong drink is a brawler, and whoever is led astray by it is not wise" (verse 1). There is no better description given of wine. It is a "mocker." Its promises are false and deceptive. People argue for the approval for moderate drinking, but no man knows or can know at what point he keeps within the limits of moderation. The results of experience demonstrate that moderation never has and never can fight intemperance successfully. What we are sure of is the soundness of the principle of abstinence. Alcoholism is a problem out of control and God only knows the degradation and misery that is caused by this deadly beverage. Child abuse, broken homes, accidents on highways and in the air and the list could continue. Today we have tried to sophisticate its use but it still remains a deadly beverage. Statistics prove this. The New Testament teaches that, that which causes others to stumble we should refrain from.

"Who can say, 'I have made my heart clean, I am pure from my sin'?" (verse 9). This could be explained to mean: Who can say this appropriately and truthfully, emphasizing the word "I" as opposed to what God's grace does for those who seek help from Him without boastfully proclaiming what they have done themselves.

"Even a child is known by his deeds, whether what he does is pure and right" (verse 11). What a child is now and what he will become later in life can often be determined by tendencies displayed as he is growing. Earliest actions are prophecies of the future. I qualify this as being a minus or plus. Minus God, tendencies toward uncleanness and evil are human nature. Plus God, each of our lives share in a miracle of transformation by His mercy and grace. Tendencies we observe in our children demand our love, care, and nurture in training and guiding them in the right way.

"It is good for nothing, cries the buyer; but when he has gone his way, then he boasts" (verse 14). Dishonesty in business and pressuring people to buy a misrepresentation of a product is much too common. We see it every day in the business world. Selling a product for much more than it is worth to make the highest profit whether the product is honestly worth it or not. The business world has lost its conscience and heart on the overcharge system. It has an uncontrolled chain-reaction to products and services. God gives warning in His Word about the falseness and unfairness that has made men selfish money-mongers because our system demands it.

"The glory of young men is their strength, and the splendor of old men is their gray head" (verse 29). Young men have a strong pulse of life and action. They can do and dare, toil and fight as no other can, and this is their glory. The apostle John wrote, *"I have written to you, young men, because you are strong"* (John 2:14). They are to be strong in courage, in a brave, resolute purpose which teaches us to hope great things, and attempt great things and never despair in God's work. Young men are to be strong in sobriety, self-control and to be sober-minded. Passions and appetites must be mastered or they will master them. It is a prime element of moral strength. Is it any wonder that today Satan strikes hardest at our youth? Without them we are a weak society and nation. They are our future. What will our world be like if drugs, alcohol and disease continue on their destructive course?

IV. Proverbs 21

"The king's heart is in the hand of the Lord, like the rivers of water; He turns it wherever He wishes" (verse 1). God can turn the influences of kings into channels of blessing. He used Cyrus, the Persian king, for blessings upon His captive children in Babylon. He makes even the wrath of kings praise Him. *"To do righteousness and justice is more acceptable to the Lord than sacrifice"* (verse 3). It is our duty to God to do justice and show love to our neighbor. This is more pleasing to God than our offerings and our sacrifices.

"A haughty look, a proud heart, and the plowing of the wicked are sin" (verse 4). A high look and a proud heart are repulsive to God because they are manifestations of a spirit that disowns His supreme authority and disregards the law of love to man.

Verse six shows the folly of those that hope to enrich themselves by dishonest practices. God requires truth on the lips and justice in the balance. The use of deceit to gain a worldly advantage has left a poor witness to the world and a blot on the lives of professing Christians and a weakening moral influence on the Church.

"There is desirable treasure, and oil in the dwelling of the wise, but a foolish man squanders it" (verse 20). The wise man will secure ample provision for his household; the foolish man will use all he has instead of putting part of it in savings. The wise lay up for the future.

"Whoever guards his mouth and tongue keeps his soul from troubles" (verse 23). Many of our problems come from the abuse of the tongue. Solomon guarantees exemption from most of the problems to one who discreetly governs that unruly member. He that offends not in word is a perfect man. Speech is a sacred prerogative: the tongue rules the word and we should take care that our hearts rule it.

"He covets greedily all day long, but the righteous gives and does not spare" (verse 26). A greedy person is content with the possession of material goods. The possession of what he wants often justifies the means by which he gets it. By a strange infatuation greed looks upon gold as its own end. The very term miser is a confession of the misery which is part of covetousness. In order to save his gold, the miser robs himself. He cannot be said to possess wealth —it possesses him. Many obsessions are abandoned as age and experience increase, but greediness strikes deeper roots, as a general rule of life, as people get older. In making this choice he heaps a world of care upon himself, yet many changes may come and intervene between his passion and its object.

V. Proverbs 22

"A good name is to be chosen rather than great riches, loving favor rather than silver and gold" (verse 1). A good name is precious and is to be chosen above wealth and precious metal. A good name and favor are won by the kind of person you are. They are earned, not bought.

"The rich and the poor have this in common, the Lord is the maker of them all" (verse 2). We are the creatures of the same hand, the subjects of the same government, we occupy the same economy of Divine providence and grace. The rich and the poor have existed in every society. The Bible does not teach communism; it does teach brotherhood with a recognition of the right relationship toward God and between man. Work, help and love is the teaching of the Bible and needs to be implemented to meet the needs of our society. With Christ there is no difference among classes any more than among nationalities. The rich are essential to the poor; the poor to the rich. God is the maker of them all. Rich and poor are equal when they stand at the foot of the Redeemer's cross asking forgiveness and pardon for their sins; seeking His righteousness to cover their uncleanness. They are equal when they come before God to worship. They are equal when both shall stand before the judgment seat of Christ. Riches are no reproach and poverty is no merit. The pride in either the rich or poor, God reproves. The level of what a man possesses is not in the category of material things only. A poor man can be rich because of what he is spiritually. His life is not so cluttered with earthly possessions. The same is true of wealth. Many people with wealth share freely in the work of Christ considering treasures in heaven of greater value than what they possess here. They use their wealth to the glory and honor of Christ.

"By humility and the fear of the Lord are riches and honor and life" (verse 4). We recognize that the whole life is the work of Divine grace; and while pride claims merit for self, and therefore goes before a fall, humility confesses day by day, *"by the grace of God I am what I am"* (I Cor. 15:10). Humility is the condition and guarantee of grace.

"Train up a child in the way he should go, and when he is old he will not depart from it" (verse 6). Training a child may be said to consist in four things: true teaching, discipline, example, and prayer. The teaching of truth concerns its relationship to God and man. Supply truth to the minds of your children. Let them know all that is right to do, both with respect to God and man. To tell a child what to do is a valuable thing but to show how it is done is far more valuable. The power of example is the power of character. Prayer -You are not alone in this work. Endeavor to guide your children in spiritual values. God is concerned for the welfare of your children. Seek His help and guidance. Children are His gifts to you and are meant to be a blessing. Let your children know from you as a parent, that the Good Shepherd loves them, is watching over them with kindly care. He knows their name and wants them to follow Him. Fathers and mothers should both understand and remember that no one can take their place in the lives of their children. Rejected by one parent or the other leaves a child scarred for life. Broken homes are never a solution. How much better to nurture a forgiveness than to forsake God given responsibilities in your children. God is in the mending business if you will seek His help for a disturbed or broken home.

Verse 17 is the beginning of a third part of the Book of Proverbs. This part closes with Chapter 24. The writer invites attention to the words of wisdom which he has to speak; words in season fitly spoken.

"Have I not written to you excellent things of counsels and knowledge, that I may make you know the certainty of the words of truth, that you may answer words of truth to those who send to you?" (verse 20-21). It is important to know not only the words of truth but also the certainty of them, that we may grow in our faith. The Bible reveals, it does not suggest; it declares, it does not investigate. The Bible, as the inspired Word of God, is the ultimate standard and the infallible rule of faith and practice. It is known to be the Word of God not only by its internal contents and character and by the consciousness of the individual believer, but by like consciousness, the sanctified judgment, and the testimony of the whole family of God, the fruits of practical faith and earnest continuous consecrations of the moral and

spiritual ends of its high calling. The Bible is the church's text book and guide.

"Do you see a man who excels in his work? He will stand before kings; he will not stand before unknown men" (verse 29). Such men as Joseph and Daniel held positions of high responsibilities because they were diligent in business. It was certainly by strange paths that they held these positions but they were God appointed. They were the best in their service to the ungodly rulers whom they served. They were energetic, honest and diligent.

VI. Proverbs 23

Verses 1-3: "Consider carefully" not so much as "what is before you" as **who is before you**. Solomon exhorts us to consider thoughtfully where we are, in whose presence we are sitting, and how much may depend on the impression we may make upon him by our manner at his luxurious table.

Verses 4 and 5 are an admonition against making riches the chief end of one's labor. Solomon assumed that the supreme pursuit of wealth was sure to fail. *"Will you set your eyes on that which is not? For riches certainly make themselves wings; they fly away like an eagle toward heaven."*

The next three verses are also connected. Verses 6-8 are a warning against men who flatter but are deceitful, who show special favors only to mislead you and to put you off your guard. When the real purpose of their courtesies are known, it will be a sickening situation (verse 8).

From verses 15 to 35 there is another continuous collection of exhortations.

"Buy the truth, and do not sell it, also wisdom and instruction and understanding" (verse 23). Obtain truth and prize it so highly that no consideration will be given to parting with it. Its value is above rubies. We cannot obtain truth without cost. Keep truth as what you profess. It is the anchor of your hope and that which guides you. Bind it upon the palms of your hands that all your work will be done for God's glory. Write it between your eyes, that all your thoughts may be enlightened. Write it on your door posts of your doors and your gates. Keep it in your heart.

"My son, give me your heart, and let your eyes observe my ways" (verse 26). Christ's demands are not only for the surrender of the heart, but for the giving up of self and turning your life completely over to Him. To die to self is the path to living in Christ. We possess ourselves only when we give ourselves to Him. *"I have been crucified with Christ; it is no longer I who live, but Christ lives in me"* (Galatians 2:20). The heart's offering to Him is the beginning of all righteousness, He who knows us has ordained that our spiritual life will grow strong.

Verses 27, 28 gives warning against the strange woman who tries to seduce man to fall in her ditch of sensuality. Men need to be careful of the seductive woman. The Bible warns about them and the awful consequences of yielding to their invitation. In the first place, men are admonished not to even look so as to be entrapped with their enticements. These women are marked by the way they walk and look. No form of sin holds its victims with more unyielding grasp than this.

Verses 29 to 35 is a third class of texts, where wine and its effects form the principle subject. Other Old Testament references are Proverbs 31:4-5; Isaiah 5:11; Isaiah 28:1, 3, 7, 8; Jeremiah 35:1-19; Daniel 1:8; Hosea 4:11; Joel 1:5; Amos 6:6. This whole chapter is filled with warnings against the leading forms of sensual indulgence and earnest counsels to a temperate and virtuous life. The climax of this chapter deals with drunkenness in all its awful aspects. Woe, sorrow, contentions, complaining, wounds without cause, redness of eyes. All from one single unrestrained appetite. This evil today, this monster of intemperance, makes misery, anguish, unhappy homes, poverty, crime, murder and self-destruction. Christ is the only one who can truly give deliverance from the desire for intemperance.

VII. Proverbs 24

"Do not be envious of evil men, nor desire to be with them" (verse 1). God's children can never have any good reason for being envious of the prosperity of the wicked. There is a caution about having close friendships with them because of the consequences of social influence.

Verses 11 and 12: One translation puts it this way, *"Deliver those who are drawn toward death, and hold back those stumbling to the slaughter. If you say, surely we did not know this, does not He who weighs the hearts consider it? He who keeps your soul, does He not know it? And will He not render to each man according to his deeds?"* The innocent and helpless are seen being dragged to their death: the voice of God comes through the inspired proverb — "Rush to the rescue!" If you should say, *"I was a stranger and you did not take Me in, naked and you did not clothe Me, sick and in prison and you did not visit Me"* (Mat. 25:43). That man is a stranger, we know him not; of what concern is his case to me? Will not God discern your selfish heart and rebuke your lying lips and hold you to a solemn responsibility to protect mistreated humanity? It is impossible to live in this world and escape responsibility. Sometimes selfishness causes us to neglect our responsibility in helping others when they are in need.

"Do not fret because of evildoers, nor be envious of the wicked" (verses 19-20). There is no reason to fret or envy the wicked, they have no reward and no hope for a blessed future.

"Prepare your outside work, make it fit for yourself in the field; and afterward build your house." This could be interpreted as a warning against a hasty marriage. The young man is taught to cultivate his land before he has the responsibility of a wife and family. In other words, provision must be made if one is to increase responsibility.

"Do not say, I will do to him just as he has done to me; I will render to the man according to his work" (verse 29). Personal retaliation assumes to take the administration of justice out of God's hands and indicates lack of confidence in His justice. The Lord says, *"Vengeance is Mine; I will repay"* (Rom. 12:19).

"A little sleep, a little slumber, a little folding of the hands to rest; so shall your poverty come like a prowler, and your need like an armed man" (verses 33-34). Laziness and procrastination sleeps and dreams life away. This is his law of life. The sense of present duty is neglected. This too has its consequences both physically and spiritually.

Daily Bible Study Questions for Group Discussion

Note: Read notes and Scripture references before answering the questions. Some questions are for those more advanced in Bible Study. Try to answer all questions but don't be discouraged if some seem a little hard. Unless otherwise instructed, use Bible only in answering questions.

FIRST DAY: Read notes on Lesson 29.

1. What social issues are dealt with in this lesson that are still very much a concern for us today?

2. What part of the scripture text or in the notes would you have liked a little more clarification?

3. What did you find most interesting or most helpful to you from either the notes or the lecture?

4. If you were going to lecture on this group of proverbs what, subject would you focus on, and to what group of people would you like to give it?

SECOND DAY: Read Proverbs 25.

5. What verses in this Chapter would have the same implication as the parable Jesus gave in **Luke 14:7-10**?

6. Underline on your text worksheets the illustrations given of the power and influence of words in **verses 8 to 25**.

7. What verse would you use in this chapter that means "don't wear out your welcome"?

THIRD DAY: Read Proverbs 26-27.

8. "Don't be a fool" is a common expression. Underline on your text worksheets the verses in **Chapter 26** that reinforce this familiar expression.

9. Using **verses 18 to 25 in Chapter 26 and verses 1-2 in Chapter 27** underline the various kinds of wrong speech.

10. What direction for wise living do you find in **Proverbs 27:5-22**, especially in regards to friendship?

11. In the **last verses of Chapter 27**, what is the reward of diligence?

FOURTH DAY: Read Proverbs 28-29.

12. Underline on your worksheet the phrases in each verse of these chapters which give a contrast between the righteous and the wicked. (It would be good to use one color pen for the righteous and one for the wicked.)

13. There are several verses in these two chapters that give the importance of (1) keeping the law and (2) a right attitude toward the poor. Locate these and list below.

14. Mark the verses in these two chapters that are meaningful to you.

FIFTH DAY: Read Proverbs 30.

15. This chapter is written by Agur. What two things does he petition God for?

16. What four generations are mentioned and do they exist today? Give verses.

17. In **verses 24 to 28** there are three or four creatures mentioned. What lessons may we learn from them?

SIXTH DAY: Read Proverbs 31.

18. What are the three virtues the mother of King Lemuel urged upon her son?

19. Make a list of the qualities of the ideal wife as given in **verses 10 to 31**.

20. What is the one characteristic that makes all else of value in the life of a virtuous woman?

Proverbs 25

25:1 These also are proverbs of Solomon which the men of Hezekiah king of Judah copied:

2 It is the glory of God to conceal a matter, But the glory of kings is to search out a matter.

3 As the heavens for height and the earth for depth, So the heart of kings is unsearchable.

4 Take away the dross from silver, And it will go to the silversmith for jewelry.

5 Take away the wicked from before the king, And his throne will be established in righteousness.

6 Do not exalt yourself in the presence of the king, And do not stand in the place of the great;

7 For it is better that he say to you, "Come up here," Than that you should be put lower in the presence of the prince, Whom your eyes have seen.

8 Do not go hastily to court; For what will you do in the end, When your neighbor has put you to shame?

9 Debate your case with your neighbor, And do not disclose the secret to another;

10 Lest he who hears it expose your shame, And your reputation be ruined.

11 A word fitly spoken is like apples of gold In settings of silver.

12 Like an earring of gold and an ornament of fine gold Is a wise rebuker to an obedient ear.

13 Like the cold of snow in time of harvest Is a faithful messenger to those who send him, For he refreshes the soul of his masters.

14 Whoever falsely boasts of giving Is like clouds and wind without rain.

15 By long forbearance a ruler is persuaded, And a gentle tongue breaks a bone.

16 Have you found honey? Eat only as much as you need, Lest you be filled with it and vomit.

17 Seldom set foot in your neighbor's house, Lest he become weary of you and hate you.

18 A man who bears false witness against his neighbor Is like a club, a sword, and a sharp arrow.

19 Confidence in an unfaithful man in time of trouble Is like a bad tooth and a foot out of joint.

20 Like one who takes away a garment in cold weather, And like vinegar on soda, Is one who sings songs to a heavy heart.

21 If your enemy is hungry, give him bread to eat; And if he is thirsty, give him water to drink;

22 For so you will heap coals of fire on his head, And the LORD will reward you.

23 The north wind brings forth rain, And a backbiting tongue an angry countenance.

24 It is better to dwell in a corner of a housetop, Than in a house shared with a contentious woman.

25 As cold water to a weary soul, So is good news from a far country.

26 A righteous man who falters before the wicked Is like a murky spring and a polluted well.

27 It is not good to eat much honey; So to seek one's own glory is not glory.

28 Whoever has no rule over his own spirit Is like a city broken down, without walls.

Proverbs 26

26:1 As snow in summer and rain in harvest, So honor is not fitting for a fool.

2 Like a flitting sparrow, like a flying swallow, So a curse without cause shall not alight.

3 A whip for the horse, A bridle for the donkey, And a rod for the fool's back.

4 Do not answer a fool according to his folly, Lest you also be like him.

5 Answer a fool according to his folly, Lest he be wise in his own eyes.

6 He who sends a message by the hand of a fool Cuts off his own feet and drinks violence.

7 Like the legs of the lame that hang limp Is a proverb in the mouth of fools.

8 Like one who binds a stone in a sling Is he who gives honor to a fool.

9 Like a thorn that goes into the hand of a drunkard Is a proverb in the mouth of fools.

10 The great God who formed everything Gives the fool his hire and the transgressor his wages.

11 As a dog returns to his own vomit, So a fool repeats his folly.

12 Do you see a man wise in his own eyes? There is more hope for a fool than for him.

13 The lazy man says, "There is a lion in the road! A fierce lion is in the streets!"

14 As a door turns on its hinges, So does the lazy man on his bed.

15 The lazy man buries his hand in the bowl; It wearies him to bring it back to his mouth.

16 The lazy man is wiser in his own eyes Than seven men who can answer sensibly.

17 He who passes by and meddles in a quarrel not his own Is like one who takes a dog by the ears.

18 Like a madman who throws firebrands, arrows, and death,

19 Is the man who deceives his neighbor, And says, "I was only joking!"

20 Where there is no wood, the fire goes out; And where there is no talebearer, strife ceases.

21 As charcoal is to burning coals, and wood to fire, So is a contentious man to kindle strife.

22 The words of a talebearer are like tasty trifles, And they go down into the inmost body.

23 Fervent lips with a wicked heart Are like earthenware covered with silver dross.

24 He who hates, disguises it with his lips, And lays up deceit within himself;

25 When he speaks kindly, do not believe him, For there are seven abominations in his heart;

26 Though his hatred is covered by deceit, His wickedness will be revealed before the assembly.

27 Whoever digs a pit will fall into it, And he who rolls a stone will have it roll back on him.

28 A lying tongue hates those who are crushed by it, And a flattering mouth works ruin.

Proverbs 27

27:1 Do not boast about tomorrow, For you do not know what a day may bring forth.

2 Let another man praise you, and not your own mouth; A stranger, and not your own lips.

3 A stone is heavy and sand is weighty, But a fool's wrath is heavier than both of them.

4 Wrath is cruel and anger a torrent, But who is able to stand before jealousy?

5 Open rebuke is better Than love carefully concealed.

6 Faithful are the wounds of a friend, But the kisses of an enemy are deceitful.

7 A satisfied soul loathes the honeycomb, But to a hungry soul every bitter thing is sweet.

8 Like a bird that wanders from its nest Is a man who wanders from his place.

9 Ointment and perfume delight the heart, And the sweetness of a man's friend gives delight by hearty counsel.

10 Do not forsake your own friend or your father's friend, Nor go to your brother's house in the day of your calamity; Better is a neighbor nearby than a brother far away.

11 My son, be wise, and make my heart glad, That I may answer him who reproaches me.

12 A prudent man foresees evil and hides himself; The simple pass on and are punished.

13 Take the garment of him who is surety for a stranger, And hold it in pledge when he is surety for a seductress.

14 He who blesses his friend with a loud voice, rising early in the morning, It will be counted a curse to him.

15 A continual dripping on a very rainy day And a contentious woman are alike;

16 Whoever restrains her restrains the wind, And grasps oil with his right hand.

17 As iron sharpens iron, So a man sharpens the countenance of his friend.

18 Whoever keeps the fig tree will eat its fruit; So he who waits on his master will be honored.

19 As in water face reflects face, So a man's heart reveals the man.

20 Hell and Destruction are never full; So the eyes of man are never satisfied.

21 The refining pot is for silver and the furnace for gold, And a man is valued by what others say of him.

22 Though you grind a fool in a mortar with a pestle along with crushed grain, Yet his foolishness will not depart from him.

23 Be diligent to know the state of your flocks, And attend to your herds;

24 For riches are not forever, Nor does a crown endure to all generations.

25 When the hay is removed, and the tender grass shows itself, And the herbs of the mountains are gathered in,

26 The lambs will provide your clothing, And the goats the price of a field;

27 You shall have enough goats' milk for your food, For the food of your household, And the nourishment of your maidservants.

Proverbs 28

28:1 The wicked flee when no one pursues, But the righteous are bold as a lion.

2 Because of the transgression of a land, many are its princes; But by a man of understanding and knowledge Right will be prolonged.

3 A poor man who oppresses the poor Is like a driving rain which leaves no food.

4 Those who forsake the law praise the wicked, But such as keep the law contend with them.

5 Evil men do not understand justice, But those who seek the LORD understand all.

6 Better is the poor who walks in his integrity Than one perverse in his ways, though he be rich.

7 Whoever keeps the law is a discerning son, But a companion of gluttons shames his father.

8 One who increases his possessions by usury and extortion Gathers it for him who will pity the poor.

9 One who turns away his ear from hearing the law, Even his prayer is an abomination.

10 Whoever causes the upright to go astray in an evil way, He himself will fall into his own pit; But the blameless will inherit good.

11 The rich man is wise in his own eyes, But the poor who has understanding searches him out.

12 When the righteous rejoice, there is great glory; But when the wicked arise, men hide themselves.

13 He who covers his sins will not prosper, But whoever confesses and forsakes them will have mercy.

14 Happy is the man who is always reverent, But he who hardens his heart will fall into calamity.

15 Like a roaring lion and a charging bear Is a wicked ruler over poor people.

16 A ruler who lacks understanding is a great oppressor, But he who hates covetousness will prolong his days.

17 A man burdened with bloodshed will flee into a pit; Let no one help him.

18 Whoever walks blamelessly will be saved, But he who is perverse in his ways will suddenly fall.

19 He who tills his land will have plenty of bread, But he who follows frivolity will have poverty enough!

20 A faithful man will abound with blessings, But he who hastens to be rich will not go unpunished.

21 To show partiality is not good, Because for a piece of bread a man will transgress.

22 A man with an evil eye hastens after riches, And does not consider that poverty will come upon him.

23 He who rebukes a man will find more favor afterward Than he who flatters with the tongue.

24 Whoever robs his father or his mother, And says, "It is no transgression," The same is companion to a destroyer.

25 He who is of a proud heart stirs up strife, But he who trusts in the LORD will be prospered.

26 He who trusts in his own heart is a fool, But whoever walks wisely will be delivered.

27 He who gives to the poor will not lack, But he who hides his eyes will have many curses.

28 When the wicked arise, men hide themselves; But when they perish, the righteous increase.

Proverbs 29

29:1 He who is often rebuked, and hardens his neck, Will suddenly be destroyed, and that without remedy.

2 When the righteous are in authority, the people rejoice; But when a wicked man rules, the people groan.

3 Whoever loves wisdom makes his father rejoice, But a companion of harlots wastes his wealth.

4 The king establishes the land by justice, But he who receives bribes overthrows it.

5 A man who flatters his neighbor Spreads a net for his feet.

6 By transgression an evil man is snared, But the righteous sings and rejoices.

7 The righteous considers the cause of the poor, But the wicked does not understand such knowledge.

8 Scoffers set a city aflame, But wise men turn away wrath.

9 If a wise man contends with a foolish man, Whether the fool rages or laughs, there is no peace.

10 The bloodthirsty hate the blameless, But the upright seek his well-being.

11 A fool vents all his feelings, But a wise man holds them back.

12 If a ruler pays attention to lies, All his servants become wicked.

13 The poor man and the oppressor have this in common: The LORD gives light to the eyes of both.

14 The king who judges the poor with truth, His throne will be established forever.

15 The rod and rebuke give wisdom, But a child left to himself brings shame to his mother.

16 When the wicked are multiplied, transgression increases; But the righteous will see their fall.

17 Correct your son, and he will give you rest; Yes, he will give delight to your soul.

18 Where there is no revelation, the people cast off restraint; But happy is he who keeps the law.

19 A servant will not be corrected by mere words; For though he understands, he will not respond.

20 Do you see a man hasty in his words? There is more hope for a fool than for him.

21 He who pampers his servant from childhood Will have him as a son in the end.

22 An angry man stirs up strife, And a furious man abounds in transgression.

23 A man's pride will bring him low, But the humble in spirit will retain honor.

24 Whoever is a partner with a thief hates his own life; He swears to tell the truth, but reveals nothing.

25 The fear of man brings a snare, But whoever trusts in the LORD shall be safe.

26 Many seek the ruler's favor, But justice for man comes from the LORD.

27 An unjust man is an abomination to the righteous, And he who is upright in the way is an abomination to the wicked.

Notes

Notes

Proverbs 25 - 31

I. Proverbs 25

A new and later section of the Book of Proverbs begins with chapter 25. *"These also are proverbs of Solomon which the men of Hezekiah king of Judah copied"*(verse 1). Very interesting and remarkable words. They tell us of the existence of a collection of proverbs already recognized as authoritative. The sayings are the same in length, they have the same parallelism of structure and are grouped together in the same way. The men who produced this literary work were no doubt literary courtiers and friends of King Hezekiah, who copied and compiled them as we now have them.

"It is the glory of God to conceal a matter, but the glory of kings is to search out a matter" (verse 2). That God's ways are unsearchable is one of His high prerogatives. Isaiah says, *"Truly You are God, who hide Yourself, O God of Israel, the Savior!"* (Isaiah 45:15). His wisdom is that which belongs to Him as the Fountain of wisdom, the Father of light, the Source of all knowledge. *"Oh, the depth of the riches both of the wisdom and knowledge of God! How unsearchable are His judgments and His ways past finding out!"* (Romans 11:33).

"Do not go hastily to court; for what will you do in the end, when your neighbor has put you to shame?" (verse 8). A man hasty in strife or easily provoked, who readily gets into a quarrel when he is put to shame often becomes enraged and may act in a desperate manner.

"Debate your case with your neighbor, and do not disclose the secret to another; lest he who hears it expose your shame, and your reputation be ruined" (verses 9 and 10). Do not reveal secrets for the one to whom it is told will have resentment toward you for telling it. Your reputation as a secret revealer will not be forgotten.

"A word fitly spoken is like apples of gold In settings of silver" (verse 11). Words need to be spoken wisely and at the right time. There is a time to speak and a time to be silent. Silence is golden when you are angry; for if you speak then you most certainly will regret what you said in anger.

"Whoever falsely boasts of giving is like clouds and wind without rain" (verse 14). Clouds and wind sometimes promise rain, and do not give it. The boasting man promises his so called gift; but he does not keep his promise.

Have you found honey? Eat only as much as you need, lest you be filled with it and vomit" (verse 16). What the Bible forbids is excess in pleasures that come from over indulgence and lead to sin. Over-eating can also be sinful. It is harmful to your body, and time, money and effort to deal with the problems that result in this indulgence can be very costly. It is something to think about and consider carefully. To have a picture of starving people which keeps a visual image focused on the results of over eating, could be better than a diet program. There is a point at which pleasure becomes pain. If eating is to continue as pleasure, it must be enjoyed moderately. Some of our psychological problems come because we don't look good, we don't feel good and walking and exercise are too much effort. We become depressed and limited in activity because we aren't what we want to be and we can't do what we want to do. Quit worrying about yourself and start to work on your problem. Worry magnifies the situation and makes you sick, "and vomit it," bears out this interpretation.

Verse 17, says to us that if you take advantage of your friends you lose them. The meaning of verse 19 is that a treacherous man will not only fail you in a time of distress, but will annoy you like a broken tooth or a sprained foot.

Verses 21 and 22 should be together. To give bread to your enemy when he is hungry, water when he is thirsty, represents the very act of kindness and love. The thought is: love your enemies and show it by doing good to them. It requires us to think of the effect of kindness, as shown by a man to his enemies. Paul says in Romans 12:20-21, *"for in so doing you will heap coals of fire on his head. Do not be overcome by evil, but overcome evil with good."* The same doctrine of morality, the same law of love is taught in both the Old and New Testament.

"A righteous man who falters before the wicked is like a murky spring and a polluted well"(verse 26). The scandalous fall of a good man is like a bag of poison cast into the spring from which the city is supplied with water. You little realize the far reaching affect this has. Christian character must harmonize with his profession.

II. Proverbs 26

Sometimes a man is honored or respected on the basis of his personal appearance, mental abilities, his worldly possessions or his lineage and social position. The true authorized basis for honor and respect for man is his moral goodness. "Snow in summer and rain in harvest" is getting good things at the wrong time. The tendency is to rob the agriculturist of the rewards of his labor and would ultimately bring famine. It is also wrong to give honor and respect to people who are destitute of moral goodness. A good thing given but unseasonable. Verse eight of this chapter expresses the same truth.

"Like a flitting sparrow, like a flying swallow, so a curse without cause shall not alight" (verse 2). This verse seems to have reference to curses pronounced by man without cause, as the bird or sparrow, by wandering, and as the swallow, by flying, shall not come or not reach us or come upon us in the way of injury, so it is with a causeless curse. It will do no more harm than the bird that flies overhead. Goliath's curse on David is an example.

"A whip for the horse, a bridle for the donkey, and a rod for the fool's back" (verse 3). This refers to a means of keeping control of one that otherwise would be hard to handle. The application of force is needed for control. *"Do not answer a fool according to his folly, lest you also be like him. Answer a fool according to his folly, lest he be wise in his own eyes"* (verses 4-5). The connecting words "according to" are used in two different senses.

"Do not answer a fool according to his folly, lest you also be like him." Answer him according to the nature of his folly so as to refute it. Both are correct.

"Do you see a man wise in his own eyes? There is more hope for a fool than for him" (verse 12). There is no greater evidence of a man's weakness than self-conceit, and it is well said "there is more hope of a fool than of him." The more a man knows the more conscious he is of how much more he needs to learn and the more humble and unassuming he will be. Men who seek recognition are often not worthy of it, men whose worth entitles them to recognition have no need to seek it. *". . .He who humbles himself will be exalted"* (Luke 14:11), but *"the lofty looks of man shall be"* (Isa.2:11). The conceited man has only one ardent admirer, and that is himself. No trait of character conveys a more unfavorable impression on others. It is one phase of selfishness. Humility is the quality which leads men to serve others; conceit, the quality which leads them to serve themselves.

Verses 18 and 19 go together *"Like a madman who throws firebrands, arrows, and death, is the man who deceives his neighbor, and says, 'I was only joking!'"* Truth is of too much value to be passed off in jesting. Lying and slandering in jest or a false report used as a joke is no less deceitful simlpy because it was spoken in a spirit of frolic or jesting. Words are as firebrands, arrows, and death. It is false representation, and after it is said the jester says, "I was only kidding" or "It's just a joke," or "It is a sport."

Haman's gallows for Mordecai in the Book of Esther, and the enemies of Daniel, who were devoured in the lion's den after they had plotted against him illustrates the 27th. verse. *"Whoever digs a pit will fall into it, and he who rolls a stone will have it roll back on him."* By injuring others we are ourselves often the greatest sufferers.

"A lying tongue hates those who are crushed by it, and a flattering mouth works ruin" (verse 28). Flattery is deceiving and has the potential of creating vanity and self-conceit. Sometimes this is under the guise of trying to build self-esteem that we hear so much about. Flattery can produce a false image in the mind of a child. Self-esteem is not produced by flattery but is built on truthfulness. Life is built on ups and downs and we need to be able to deal with both. When on the "down" a child needs a little more love from parents so he can handle that day more positively.

III. Proverbs 27

In this proverb "boast" is the expressive word. *"Do not boast about tomorrow, for you do not know what a day may bring forth"* (verse 1). This does not forbid preparing for tomorrow. Each day is a little life and our whole life is but a day repeated. Don't lose or misspend a day. Each day is precious and its treasured goods should be anticipated. Each day should be a recognition of God as the Owner and Giver. Our responsibility is to use it with care. He gives us each day to live, work and enjoy.

"Let another man praise you, and not your own mouth; a stranger, and not your own lips" (verse 2). There are times when an encouraging word would be of more value than the richest material gift. Some are far too afraid of the effect of a little generous and well timed praise. All their flowers are kept in an ice-house. Letting in a little sunshine into the lives of others would be good. Praise is both right and useful. There are families in which it would do a world of good. There are faithful wives whose fidelity their husbands appreciate but they neglect to tell them. There are children who would be happier if their parents cheered them with a hearty "well done." There are excellent ministers who would preach better and be better pastors if their people were more likely to offer the encouragement that is due them. There is comfort and help through intelligent and discriminating praise which shows a sympathetic appreciation of our best endeavors. There is only discomfort to any true man or woman in any other praise than this. This distinction should be in our minds in all giving or receiving of praise.

"Wrath is cruel and anger a torrent, but who is able to stand before jealousy?"(verse 4). When either partner in the marriage bond becomes jealous of the other, and the warmest and most sacred sensibilities known to the human heart are violated and outraged, who can stand before this fury? Jealousy is a monster that needs to be controlled or it can result in totally irrational behavior.

Verses five and six go together. *"Open rebuke is better than love carefully concealed. Faithful are the wounds of a friend, but the kisses of an enemy are deceitful."* The friend who does not conceal my faults, warns me kindly, reproves me affectionately, even when I fall short of my duty, is my friend. Even though sometimes misunderstood, a friend admonishes and reproves for our good; but an enemy gives nothing but kisses that he may keep his victim unsuspicious and unguarded and later strike the blow. Friends and friendships are choice possessions. Let us nurture loyal and good friends.

"My son, be wise, and make my heart glad, that I may answer him who reproaches me" (verse 11). Society generally holds the father somewhat responsible for the morals of his son and if he has not done his parental duty he will be reproached for his neglect and failure. Solomon says, "Remember, my son, that my reputation as well as yours is at stake, therefore, be wise and save me from reproach."

In verses 23-27 the verses are closely connected. If you look well to your farm, it will produce what you want for food or clothing. Your supplies of food will be sufficient for all your house.

IV. Proverbs 28

"He who covers his sins will not prosper, but whoever confesses and forsakes them will have mercy"(verse 13). There is a covering of sin that proves a curse. Covering can be to avoid confession of sin or can be for the purpose of denying it. Sin is sometimes covered by a lie or an attempt to justify ourselves. All these are evil coverings and God says you will not prosper. The blessed covering of sin is by forgiveness. Confession of sin results in peace with God.

"A ruler who lacks understanding is a great oppressor, but he who hates covetousness will prolong his days" (verse 16). Covetousness consists of self-love and self-care and has little respect to any law of God or of man which gets in its way. It has no conscience as to how much may be violated to get what it wants. God has promised long life and blessing to those who hate the sin of covetousness.

"A faithful man will abound with blessings, but he who hastens to be rich will not go unpunished" (verse 20). The faithful man is a man of integrity. He will be great and rich in blessings. To get rich quick is a passion that demands all to come to the aid of fulfilling the obsession. Determined to succeed, it overlooks morality and integrity and thinks only of pursuing any means to meet his goals. Gambling, risky speculations, and hasty adventures mingled with fraud are only hurtful in their effect upon the character. They disregard all principles. One who desires wealth for its own sake will be disposed to injustice. The unjust balance and the short weight will be found in the possession of a covetous man. He is prone to take advantage of the weakness or generosity of others. This results in the ruin of character, damaged fortunes, and destroyed hopes.

"He who gives to the poor will not lack, but he who hides his eyes will have many curses" (verse 27). What we give to the poor we deliver and intrust unto God's hands. The liberal man, in giving, will ever be rich. God's love and favor are his reward, and God's Word is his assurance. "Hiding the eyes" here is closing one's own eyes so that he cannot see the suffering humanity about him nor the miseries of the poor.

V. Proverbs 29

These final instructions cover subjects in the previous chapters. *"He who is often rebuked, and hardens his neck, will suddenly be destroyed, and that without remedy"* (verse 1). God has spoken to us through His Word. Examples of hardening the heart are found in Pharaoh, Ahab, and others who have rejected the instructions given in God's Word.

"A man who flatters his neighbor spreads a net for his feet" (verse 5). Flattery so often has a tendency for hypocrisy. The motive for flattery should

be considered and one needs to abstain from anything that may not be truth.

In verse 23 it says, *"a man's pride will bring him low, but the humble in spirit will retain honor."* Pride is an overestimate of our importance. Humility, on the other hand, is a willingness to take the place which God has given us, not envying those who hold higher positions or looking down on those below us.

This chapter concludes the proverbs of Solomon. The instructions which he received from the Lord for his conduct and life, for his guidance and direction, were given to him to give to others. One chapter of this special book of instructions should be read each day.

VI. Proverbs 30

This chapter and the next are not Solomon's; but this one of Agur and the next of Lemuel from his mother. The questions in verse 4 contemplate God as seen in the glory and majesty of His works of creation.

Verses 5 and 6: Out of the consciousness of the importance of all man's efforts after the knowledge of God, there is a sense of the preciousness of every living word that God has Himself revealed. We may be sure that every word He utters will be pure. *"Every word of God is pure; He is a shield to those who put their trust in Him. Do not add to His words, lest He rebuke you, and you be found a liar."*

In verses 7 to 9 Agur prays for two things: **first**, put vanity and lies far from my heart; let my spirit never be polluted, even in the sight of God, with falsehood, and **second**, of earthly goods let me have a simple competence. Not more, lest becoming over-fed, I lose the sense of my dependence upon God and say in guilty pride, "Who is the Lord? And what do I need from Him?" Or lest I be poor and steal, and profane the name of my God.

Verses 11 to 14 specify four classes of people, each one dependent on the other. The **first** is of children who curse their parents; the **second** of hypocrites and self-pleasers; the **third** of proud men, who are exalted in their own opinions, the **fourth** of cruel oppressors who kill and devour the poor.

Verses 15-16: Critics mostly agree that the word "horseleach" (KJV) represents fiction of ancient mythology of a bloodsucker creature who supposedly visited the desert and fastened upon its victims by night to suck their blood. With this, the writer compares four other things. In verse 16, the grave, the barren womb, water and fire. These perhaps represent those who are never satisfied and have a craving appetite that always cries out for more. They will always be wanting.

Verses 24 to 28 give a group of four small creatures. Each in his way seem to be wise. They each suggest what man might do if he were to give himself earnestly to the study and practice of the wisdom for which God has given him the capacity.

1. The ants know the time of their opportunity and make the best of it.

2. The conies represent a feeble folk. The tenant is weak; the habitation is strong. It is something like our rabbit in size, figure and color.

3. The locusts have no king yet they come forth all of them by bands. Everyone of them has a little kingliness in himself. They represent cooperation. This is how it must be in business, families, churches and in government.

4. *"The spider skillfully grasps with its hands."* This skill has its rewards. It represents patience, and progress — getting into kings' houses and high places.

VII.   Proverbs 31

This chapter, as well as the proceeding one is unique and unlike the first 29 chapters of this book. It comes from a certain king Lemuel and his mother.

The chapter is in two parts.

1. Verses 1-9 is a wise mothers' counsel to her son with reference to his responsibilities and duties as king.
2. Verses 10-31 give the qualities and praises of a virtuous woman. The same mother's hand may be supposed to have originated both parts of this interesting chapter.

Verses 1-9. These nine verses contain the instructions of Lemuel's mother. She cautions against incontinence and drunkenness; admonitions in respect to doing justice and vindicating the oppressed. The precepts are brief but very expressive. The cautions are directed against those vices into which kings are most likely to fall. Wine, women and oppression in order to collect money from the people, are things about which kings usually need very impressive instruction. The mother gives excellent advice with great kindness and in sincere earnestness. She desired that her son rule under God for the protection and vindication of human rights.

Verses 10-31 is a description of a true and good woman consisting of twenty-two verses. This text indicates that the position of woman in the Hebrew community during this period of time was one of special honor, trust, and efficiency. This detail of her daily life shows not only the elevating tendency of Mosaic social system, but it is informative with interesting instruction concerning domestic customs and household economy. The family is large, wealthy and eminent; and this wife, mother and mistress, by her wise energetic industry, and activity, mainly is concerned with her family's prosperity and happiness. It presents a beautiful picture of the true elements of womanly excellence; what the true woman is in her home, to her husband, and children, and household and to the poor; her high, pure aim, her industry, her helpful counsel and sympathy, her care for the outward needs and the heart training of all dependent upon her.

Evaluation Review (Proverbs, Lessons 25 to 30)

FIRST DAY: **Work questions from either notes or your Bible.**

1. Name the authors of the Book of Proverbs.

2. Give illustrations from your notes of the differences between a moral sentence and a proverb.

3. What are some of the issues dealt with in the Book of Proverbs that were most outstanding to you?

SECOND DAY:

4. As you recall, what are some gems of advice given to young people that are just as relevant for today?

5. In general, how would you characterize Solomon's instructions as to the consequences of the pursuit of good over against those who turn to wicked paths?

6. From **lesson 26**, what is represented by "wisdom" in the Book of Proverbs?

THIRD DAY:

7. What does Solomon advise regarding becoming surety or being the undersigned for another's debts?

8. In **lesson 27** what is learned about the devastating effect of sensual sins and their psychological effect on people? What is God's provision and remedy?

9. Proverbs deals with the tongue and the power of speech for both good or evil. After reading **Proverbs 10**, what is to be commended in the uses of speech and what is to be avoided?

FOURTH DAY:

10. When you consider the seriousness of the tongue and speech from **lesson 28**, what should be our prayer each day?

11. What are some of the consequences of children who lack parental guidance and training by word and example?

12. Give some thoughts from **lesson 28** about a "merry heart", "being cheerful" and "laughter."

13. What is said about "the hoary head" in **Proverbs 16:31**, from the notes on **Lesson 28**?

FIFTH DAY: (Questions from Lesson 29 notes)

14. (a) What other verse in **Proverbs 18** would give the same message as the proverb *"A wounded or offended spirit is harder to be won than a walled city"* ?

    (b) Give some examples that could result in a wounded spirit.

15. In your notes on **Lesson #29, pages 2 and 3**, what did you learn from **Proverbs 19:17** about the ministry to the poor that is helpful both personally and as a church?

16. What is said about a wife in **Proverbs 18 and 19**?

SIXTH DAY:

17. What did you learn about over-indulgence in eating and pleasure in lesson #30?

18. What are the good and bad consequences to follow covering sin and confessing and forsaking sin in **Proverbs 28**?

19. What is different about **Proverbs 30 and 31** from the first twenty-nine chapters in the book?

20. What was special to you in **Proverbs 31**?

Notes

Ecclesiastes and Song of Solomon
A Synopsis

I. The Book of Ecclesiastes

A. Introduction

Although the name of Solomon is not mentioned as the author of Ecclesiastes as it is in Proverbs and the Song of Solomon, the description of the author (Ecclesiastes 1:1, 12) applies so definitely to him that it answers the purpose as if he were named.

The Book of Ecclesiastes is included as part of the Jewish sacred cannon of Scripture by the same authority as other books and endorsed by Christ and His apostles. It is a book that is *"profitable for doctrine, for reproof, for correction, for instruction in righteousness"* (II Timothy 3:16). It regards the experiments, observations, and reflections of the wise king of Israel (Solomon) as it relates to that which constitutes the true happiness and real welfare of man. Like the books of Job and Proverbs, it deals with the questions of human life from the standpoint of "wisdom", showing that not only as a matter of duty and obligation, but from a regard to his own highest interest, man should obey the law of God. These three books form a complete circle in the treatment of this common theme. Proverbs shows to us the harmony between man's duty and his true interests in the common experience of men. It sets forth the fact that righteous doing has its reward and evil doing its penalty.

The Book of Job discusses the case of a man of eminent piety, who, from no fault of his own, but at the suggestion of the Evil One, was put in a position of terrible distress. Yet God's design in it all was a gracious one and resulted in the restitution of Job's piety and the increase of his prosperity. Ecclesiastes is occupied with the opposite case: a king without equal in wisdom and prosperity, who gave himself to find satisfaction from purely worldly sources; but after the experiments of a lifetime, reached the conclusion that to fear God and keep His commandments was the whole concern of man and the only source of his true happiness and welfare. It is the confession of a man looking back upon his past life and looking out upon the disorders and calamities which surround him. The writer was a man who had sinned in giving way to selfishness and sensuality. He paid the penalty of that sin in fullness and weariness of life but through all this was under the discipline of God, and has learned from it the lessons which God meant to teach him. The writer concludes by pointing out that the secret of a true life is that a man should consecrate the vigor and vitality of his youth to God.

This book teaches the thinking mind how it must handle the problems of life and the emptiness of all human effort which is unable to solve the perplexities of our experiences. It shows how to find the only solid results available. All is vanity except our faith in a loving God who loves and cares for us. This is the "conclusion of the whole matter." Like the Book of Job, Ecclesiastes gives the struggles of a mind perplexed by certain aspects of human life. The results of these struggles lie in the lesson it would teach.

B. Subjects and Aims of the Book

It is recommended that the personal history of Solomon up to the time when he wrote this book be carefully studied. This will help in understanding his special aim and purpose in writing it. (I Chronicles 23-29), (II Chronicles 1-9). The heart of Solomon became pleasure-loving and pleasure-seeking. He sought pleasure in wealth and splendor, in fame and honor: he sought it in all forms of sensual enjoyment. Such pleasure-seeking swept him away from the fear and service of God. It led him on to those associations which ensnared him into idolatry. Only by God's gracious providence was Solomon's life spared till he experienced conviction of his sin before God and his people. He *"came to himself and thought on his ways"* and he felt the solemn obligation *"to fear God and keep His commandments"* as the duty of man. Having reached these convictions, it was inevitable that he should feel the importance of undoing the wrong he had done. Ecclesiastes also presents the fact of a future life. It dwells upon the emptiness and failure of all earthly things, the character of human events, and the impartial, irresistible onset of decay and death. These facts present an argument to enforce the necessity of a future existence, in which the unsatisfied cravings of man's heart may be met. It is only there that all problems will have fitting solutions and life may be forever unmarred by decay and not be subjected to death. It also employs the same fact to impress the reality of ultimate judgment. This book, in its direct and implied teachings really contrasts the present unreal and unsatisfying life with one that is real, abiding, progressive, and satisfying. Its chief aim is earnestly to commend such a wise, right use of life that now is, as to ensure the possession and enjoyment of that blessed life to come.

"God will judge the righteous and the wicked" (3:17). He appointed a time in which all will come under the judicial cognizance of His court of justice. There is One higher than the highest earthly ruler (5:8), One who will punish oppressors, One who will vindicate the oppressed that have no comforter here (4:1). The young may rejoice in their blessings, but they are always to keep in view the judgment to come (11:9). *"God will bring every work into judgment, including every secret thing, whether good or evil"* (12:14).

God is to be feared (3:14). Sin makes Him angry (5:6). Why feared? And what will His anger do? Those who fear God shall experience deliverance (7:18). Wickedness shall not deliver those who are given to it (8:8). *"It shall be well with them who fear God"* (8:12). *"It shall not be well with those who do not fear Him"* (8:13). *"Remember now your Creator"* (12:1); which implies reward to the obedient. *"Fear God, and keep His commandments"* (12:13). The doctrine of retribution, a time when every action will be considered and judged, is recorded through the entire Book of Ecclesiastes. Another thing to keep in mind, which is confirmed by Scripture, is that this time

of retribution, adequate and final of judgment and rewards will be given, but does not take place in this present world. Every person will be accountable for things done in this world both good and evil as we stand before the Almighty and righteous Judge of all the earth.

It makes one think soberly about life and its purpose before a God who loves us and has made provision for us in His Son, Jesus Christ. We today have opportunity for choices and are responsible before our God to trust Him and make those choices that will insure us of eternity with Him. We are not puppets in the hands of God. He has endowed each one with a free will. We make many choices every day. Let us study His Word, know what His way and will is for our lives and commit ourselves to following Him. Compare Ecclesiastes 1:1 with 12:13, 14. It is that great day when *"God shall bring every work unto judgment,"* which alone redeems "all" things; man and concerns of the world in which he spends his brief existence, from being regarded as an inexplicable mystery, or as the greatest "vanity" imaginable.

II.   The Book of the Song of Solomon

In the Hebrew, this Book is called the Song of Songs. The Jews revere the song as among the holiest of sacred books. Proverbs is compared to the outer court of the Temple, Ecclesiastes to the holy place, and the Song of Songs to the holy of holies, the inmost sanctuary of God.

The nation already had in its possession the song of Moses and Miriam at the Red Sea; the last song of Moses in review of God's loving care of His chosen people through their forty years of wandering; the Song of Deborah over the fall of Israel's foes; and many songs of the sweet Psalmist of Israel, all of which we may suppose this poem of Solomon to be compared as the Song of all songs, inferior to none.

This book is included among the sacred books by all standard authorities; endorsed by Christ and His apostles, and attributed to Solomon as its author. All other Scripture has a high moral purpose and an obvious aim. Therefore, we are obligated to look for such purpose and aim in this book of the Song of Solomon. If we may apply a figurative construction, the book speaks of a noble theme with high moral purpose. The love of God to His chosen and redeemed people. A love so pure, so deep, so true, so rich in its fruits of blessing, so fraught with reacting influence toward reciprocal love in return, what can be a more worthy theme for poetry and song?

The poem deals with the expression of the strongest passion of our nature and presents a picture of faithful love. It gives to us the warmest emotions and its simplicity and purity of enjoyment. In the secondary meaning, this book treats the subject of love as between husband and wife in pure devotion to each other. *"My beloved is mine, and I am his"* expresses the beautiful blending of the love of nature and the charms of rural life with the endearment of a wedded love relation.

There are only three main speakers in the book: "the bride," "the beloved," and a chorus of "virgins" or "daughters of Jerusalem." Love is first portrayed in its ecstatic fervor of emotion in mutual delight of the lover and the beloved. It is then celebrated as **nuptial love** in the rejoicing of the bridegroom and the bride. In the second half of the poem, from chapter 5:2 to chapter 8:14, **love is portrayed as tried**, for a time in danger of being lost, ultimately recovered and expanding into the **fullness of joy**.

The poem is divided into three parts:

1. The Rapture of First Love Chapter 1-3:5
2. Nuptial rejoicing Chapter 3:6-5:1
3. Separation and Reunion Chapter 5:2-8:14

The great central theme in this Song is that of God's relationship to His people in covenant with Himself as in the likeness to the marriage relation in human society. The bride is not necessarily the individual Christian but is considered the church as a whole.

It is true that in loving the church, God loves the individual Christian who makes up the body of Christ. We learn from this Song that the love between God and His people should be mutual. In a marriage covenant each party professes and binds itself to love the other. Love received should cause responsive love in return. So a sense of God's love to us should quicken and intensify our love for Him. One of the first lessons taught in this Song is the strength of the love which God has toward His people. The words of the text indicate the deepest and strongest love known to man.

In Ephesians, chapter 5, Paul said, *"Husbands, love your wives, just as Christ also loved the church and gave Himself for her"* (verse 25). There can be no stronger love.

So we have the deeper meaning of human love and God's Divine love expressed in this Song. God's people are His "bride." The Lord is greater than Solomon, even Christ. The spiritual element of this book must be considered and applied. The earthly theme would be the love of Solomon and Shulamith; the spiritual theme, Christ's love for His church, the covenant people of God.

Notes